HOLY FATHER

Also by Greg Tobin:

NONFICTION

Selecting the Pope: Uncovering the Mysteries of Papal Elections (2003)

*The Wisdom of St. Patrick: Inspirations from the
Patron Saint of Ireland* (1999)

*Saints and Sinners: The American Catholic Experience through Stories,
Memoirs, Essays, and Commentary* (1999)

FICTION

Conclave (2001)

Council (2002)

HOLY FATHER

Pope Benedict XVI

PONTIFF FOR A NEW ERA

Greg Tobin

STERLING PUBLISHING
New York

This book is dedicated to my editorial and bookselling colleagues at Barnes & Noble Publishing and Sterling Publishing Co., Inc. with gratitude for their support on an exciting journey.

Published by Sterling Publishing Co., Inc.
387 Park Avenue South, New York, NY 10016

© 2005 by Greg Tobin

Distributed in Canada by Sterling Publishing
c/o Canadian Manda Group, 165 Dufferin Street
Toronto, Ontario, Canada M6K 3H6

Distributed in Great Britain by Chrysalis Books
64 Brewery Road, London N7 9NT, England

Distributed in Australia by Capricorn Link (Australia) Pty. Ltd.
P.O. Box 704, Windsor, NSW 2756, Australia

ISBN 1-4027-3172-8

Library of Congress Cataloging-in-Publication Data available upon request

1 3 5 7 9 8 6 4 2

Manufactured in the United States of America

TABLE OF CONTENTS

ACKNOWLEDGMENTS

Because this book was published under rather unique circumstances, which required the editor to enforce difficult deadlines and oversee a complicated process, I wish to acknowledge and thank Meredith Peters for her extraordinary focus on all aspects of publication, from concept and writing to corrections and design. Also, I must thank J. Alan Kahn and Michael Fragnito for their commitment to this project. I extend my appreciation to many others at Barnes & Noble Publishing, including Wendy Ralphs, Jeffrey Batzli, and Charles Ryf, as well as copy editor Monique Peterson, who all worked hard and contributed much to this book.

The publishing and publicity professionals at Sterling Publishing have invested much valuable time and focus on the project. Special thanks are due to Kelly Galvin and Leigh Ann Ambrosi for their work on *Selecting the Pope*.

At Seton Hall University and Immaculate Conception Seminary, various faculty, staff, administrators, and students were helpful in ways small and very large indeed. A profound thank you is due to Monsignor Robert Sheeran, president of the university; Tom White, assistant vice president of public relations and marketing; and research assistant Michael Barone, a seminarian. Others in the Ring Building, nerve center of the public relations department, propelled me from one book to the next. And Monsignor Robert J. Wister, as before, laid the scholarly foundation for this structure to stand upon, as did Fathers Thomas Guarino and Anthony Figueiredo.

Also, colleagues and supervisors at the Archdiocese of Newark, from Archbishop John J. Myers and James Goodness, director of communications, to Marge Pearson-McCue, director of operations of *The Catholic Advocate*, and Deacon Joseph A. Dwyer, Jr., vice chancellor for administration, have been supportive to an immeasurable degree. A special thank you to Catholic News Service, as well.

My family was tolerant and more than a bit curious during the "crash" stages of the project, supplying me with coffee, meals, space, quiet, and encouragement during difficult hours. I thank Maureen, Patrick, and Bryan, as always.

INTRODUCTION

The death and funeral of Pope John Paul II brought on a worldwide outpouring of personal, spiritual emotion; millions came to Rome from all walks of life and nearly every inhabited region on the globe. A new man, Pope Benedict XVI, follows one of the most beloved, dynamic, and long-reigning pontiffs in history. And he ascends to the papal throne on a world stage in a media age that aggressively chronicled John Paul II—both in life and after death.

Indeed, after Pope John Paul's death, encomiums and criticisms immediately poured out in the print media. Television coverage continued "wall-to-wall" over the weekend and throughout the week until his funeral on Friday, April 8. In the United States, media attention shifted from sordid celebrity criminal trials and hotly contentious cultural and political issues—such as the death of Terry Schiavo in Florida—to make way for a new group of experts and commentators. Well-groomed men in Roman collars and black suits spoke in measured tones of the loss of their universal leader. Religious women—very few in traditional nuns' habits—joined the chorus of comment with somber voices and feminine insight into a world almost exclusively populated by men: the Vatican and Roman curia.

For moments in the Easter season of 2005, the papacy retained—or perhaps regained—its relevance to contemporary issues. Poverty and war did not end; billions did not convert to Catholicism; disease and death were not eradicated. Yet, the teaching and practices of the church rose to the fore of debate and discussion among Catholics, non-Catholics, and non-Christians alike.

Now, with a new leader at the helm of the Bark of St. Peter, urgent questions arise regarding the future of the Catholic Church. Will Benedict, considered by many to be staunchly conservative, help the church to maintain its doctrinal authority as well as its ecumenical agenda—both in the U.S. and abroad? Or will the two-thousand-year-old institution be weakened by further scandals, internal divisions, external threats, and continued secularization?

John Paul II certainly made the papacy relevant again to Christianity and to Christians today, whether they fully accepted the papal primacy (his preeminent position in the church) or not. A 2003 poll of American Catholics revealed the following: ninety-four percent agreed that the pope led effectively through personal holiness, eighty-eight percent thought that he had done a good job leading the worldwide church, and sixty-five percent believed that he understood "the distinctive challenges of the U.S. church." Regarding social concerns, eighty-seven percent of those polled felt that he was an effective leader in opposing abortion, eighty percent agreed he had been strong on economic justice issues and the needs of the poor—but only fifty-four percent of American Catholics expressed a positive opinion of Pope John Paul II's efforts to "improve the status of women in the church."[1]

Such a poll proves at the very least that Catholics in North America pay attention to and take seriously the Holy Father's actions. But what about Catholics around the world and non-Catholic Christians?

Many people, Christians or not, have no reason to find a connection to the church of Rome to be desirable in any way—and a certain number simply abhor such a notion. Even some Catholics might dispute the direct relevance of a Roman pontiff in their lives and the practice of their faith. John Paul II appealed to these groups in a distinct way, especially through his wide-ranging and frequent world travels. He was the most visible pope in history, a true media phenomenon in a way that his predecessors had not been—indeed could not have been before the Information Age.

Yet it is also revealing to look at how the popes of the previous fifty years (as one semi-arbitrary benchmark) profoundly affected both the church and the world. Each of them has been concerned, primarily, with the men and women who "belong" to the Catholic communion and, as such, are members of his "flock." For these recent popes, above all, have been shepherds—leaders, teachers, and protectors. They have also been temporal rulers, the sovereigns of a small state (much reduced from the time when the pope was de facto civil ruler of Rome and two-thirds of Italy), which receives ambassadors from nearly two hundred nations. But the Vatican City State is not the source of the pope's true power nor, in fact, his relevance on the world stage—though it ought not to be underestimated, either: witness the collapse of the Soviet empire and the end of the Cold War during the reign of John Paul II.

The source of the pope's power and prestige in the world resides in the moral realm, and even more deeply, in the apostolic tradition that is traced back to Jesus of Nazareth, whose teachings were handed down by the apostles who walked with him during his earthly ministry and witnessed the risen Christ afterward. Protestants oppose Catholic teaching on the papacy for relying too much on tradition versus scripture—which contains some individual references to Peter, but no explicit endorsement of apostolic succession or the papacy itself.

Yet, in the face of this critique (which is not new), how does the doctrine of apostolic succession give the pope (and all the bishops of the Catholic Church) a relevance that compels the attention of the world and obedience of the faithful? Has that claim upon human souls been exercised meaningfully, or—posed in another way—has the papal office remained, despite the buffets of time, scandal, sin, and personal weaknesses, the primary (or primatial) source of authority that it claims to be?

Somewhat mysteriously, the answer is yes. For the past two hundred years, the popes have been men of character and personal holiness, which has gone a long way toward allaying the fears and experiences of the more distant past. The popes from Pius VII to John Paul II have been, for the most part, judicious and diplomatic in public circumstances (critics would say that they were too often overcautious), both of necessity and by temperament.

The first and last time a pope exercised his infallible teaching authority since its definition by the First Vatican Council in 1870, was in 1950 when Pius XII proclaimed the doctrine of the Assumption of the Blessed Virgin Mary. A consensus among the Catholic faithful and Catholic theologians, which had grown through nineteen centuries, made the definition of this particular dogma seem a natural step for the Holy Father to take. This infrequent and cautious use of such authority is another hallmark of the modern papacy, which moves deliberately on such doctrinal developments. In contrast, Pope John Paul II, in his 2002 encyclical letter on the rosary, surprised Catholics and other observers when he created a new set of "mysteries" (meditations upon the life and ministry of Jesus) to be recited among the other prayers of the rosary. The announcement was startling and newsworthy, yet it was neither earth-shattering, nor a major doctrinal development.

Pius XII was the classic intellectual defender and explainer (apologist), the last "general" of the post-Tridentine Church Militant, who also served for an unusually long time—through World War II and the Cold War. John Paul was a bolder, busier, brighter Supreme Pastor than most of his predecessors, a man from "a far country" (as he referred to Poland's geographical and cultural distance from Rome) and he was the second-longest reigning pope on historical record. Pius may well have considered calling the bishops to council, but in the end it was his successor who convoked Vatican II. John Paul was very much a "product" of the eventual council. The two twentieth-century popes were separated by only three popes and twenty years, yet the contrast could hardly be more stark—in style, personality, and origin.

If John XXIII had not convoked the Second Vatican Council (only the twenty-first ecumenical or general council in history), how different the course of church history—and papal history—would have been. The influence of this momentous event was visible throughout John Paul's active pontificate.

On May 25, 1995, John Paul II's encyclical letter, *Ut unum sint*, articulated a new approach to the idea of the "primacy of Peter," that is, the preeminent position of the pope as the first among equals in the college of bishops, and as the "servant of Christian unity." *Ut unum sint*, meaning, "that they all may be one" (from John 17:21), is primarily a call for renewed ecumenical discussion among Catholic and non-Catholic Christians, focusing on dialogue among the churches and a consideration of the pope's role now and in the future as the symbol and necessary protector of unity among all Christians. It is a fascinating document that bears reading and rereading when reflecting on the modern—post-modern, really—papacy and how John Paul's successors may approach the ever-important issue of ecumenical dialogue among all Christians.

In the document, John Paul does not flinch from describing the vital importance of the Petrine ministry among the churches throughout history and into the future. The See of Peter is the symbol and "guarantor" of unity, as found in scripture and tradition. He says, explicitly:

> As the heir to the mission of Peter in the church, which has been made fruitful by the blood of the Princes of the Apostles, the Bishop of Rome exercises a ministry originating in the manifold mercy of God. This mercy converts hearts and pours forth the power of grace where the disciple experiences the bitter taste of his personal weakness and helplessness. The authority proper to this ministry is completely at the service of God's merciful plan and it must always be seen in this perspective. Its power is explained from this perspective.[2]

The Petrine ministry, the papacy, is not "lording" over but "keeping watch" over the "particular churches" (local dioceses) that are entrusted to other pastors (bishops), who are themselves deemed successors of the apostles. The Bishop of Rome, in this view, is thereby "the first servant of unity."[3]

In addition to *Ut unum sint*, and other historic statements, Pope John Paul II promulgated new rules for the papal election process. This latest conclave is the first to be held under the revised process; it is historic not only because it elected the successor of one of the most extraordinary popes of all time, but also because it tested provisions that had never been applied before. On February 22, 1996, John Paul II issued the encyclical *Universi Dominici Gregis*, meaning "The shepherd of the Lord's whole flock." This apostolic constitution amended the conclave procedures in some significant ways, but kept intact the basic rules that had been established in the eleventh and thirteenth centuries: that is, after the mourning and burial of the deceased pope, the cardinals meet in secret to elect a successor by a two-thirds vote of electors present.[4]

The election of a new pope promises many things, not the least of which may be a change in "style." An exceptionally long pontificate such as John Paul II's will undergo phases of development, changes in both style and substance, that a shorter reign—say, up to five or six years—will not. Witness John Paul II's first few years of exceptional vigor and stage presence, interrupted by the assassination attempt in 1981, from which he emerged a leader transformed—and from which security and health concerns mushroomed to unprecedented levels. John Paul single-handedly changed the papacy forever in respect to its level of visibility in the media (and the professionalism of the Vatican's communications) and its pastoral function within the church itself.

However, personality and intellect can carry a pontificate only so far and for so long. The new pope will inherit a bureaucracy that is legendary in its scope and power.

The Roman Curia will be a check on the newly elected pontiff, unless and until he takes the reins firmly in hand and begins to fill the key positions with his own men. For example, the Secretariat of State wields a considerable amount of power within the Holy See, and the top-ranking officials traditionally have constant access to the Holy Father. The Congregations for Bishops, Clergy, and the Doctrine of the Faith, among others, are powerful agencies that exercise authority in the name of the Holy Father. They are managed by cardinals, archbishops, and bishops who are often skilled, life-long church bureaucrats. Thus institutional pressures join with spiritual and political pressures on the man in St. Peter's Chair, placing him in a pressure cooker unlike almost any other in contemporary governmental or corporate organizations. He must be a man who is able to rise above such conflicts and constraints, as was John Paul for most of his reign, if he is to serve and to rule to his full potential.

Most importantly, perhaps, the pope is a man who operates within a distinct set of historical circumstances and requirements that are impossible to avoid. Unlike a president of the United States, the Holy Father cannot overturn political, legal, or constitutional "precedents" because *his* precedents are extra-legal, extra-constitutional, and beyond the secular-political. The pope is responsible for the protection and transmission of a sacred "deposit" of faith dating back to those who walked with Jesus himself. As powerful as he is, in ecclesiastical terms, he is not omnipotent; he is one among the College of Bishops, though distinctly the first among them. He may speak infallibly, but only to decree or define a matter of faith or morality that is already firmly established within the magisterial, traditional, and scriptural context that defines his office. In these ways he is tied directly to the apostles whose faith he teaches. And in these ways he is a part of a grand history with many yesterdays, but an unknown number of tomorrows. He is, by the nature of his office and his person, one of those apostles, and one who walks with Jesus Christ as surely as did the original Twelve.

The papacy represents continuity with and from the church of the first Pentecost when those apostles received the Holy Spirit in the wind and in tongues of fire. The Petrine ministry embodies the apostolic foundation of the churches of Rome, Jerusalem, and Antioch, of the universal church. The pope is an apostle for contemporary Catholics, just as

> [f]or the earliest Christians...the apostles were living presences, precious guarantors of truth. The apostolic churches possessed more than a pedigree, they spoke with the voices of their founders, and provided living access to their teaching. And in Rome, uniquely, the authority of two apostles converged. The charismatic voice of Paul...joined with the authority of Peter, symbol of the church's jurisdiction in both heaven and earth, the one to whom the commission to bind and to feed had been given by Christ himself.[5]

The first test of the new pope will be to establish a means, a "style" if you will, of communication within his church and with the world at large.

It is not an exaggeration to look back to the year 604, to the passing of Gregory the Great—who certainly established a style and a tone for popes for all the ages—to find a historical analogy to the current situation in the history of the papacy. Each papal election thereafter for decades was a response to Pope Gregory's legacy. He actually was not very popular in Rome at the time of his death (unlike John Paul II), thus the two transitional figures who briefly succeeded him, Sabinian and Boniface III, were first anti-, then pro-Gregory's policies. Then came Boniface IV (608–615), a disciple of Gregory, who was followed by Deusdedit (Adeodatus I, 615–618), a decidedly anti-Gregorian priest—and so it went.

John Paul's legacy, his gift, if you will, is a similar invitation to which his successors must respond. He often preached, "Do not be afraid," and Pope Benedict has quoted that admonition in his early messages. John Paul the Great (which he is already, albeit unofficially, called) bequeathed the task of continuing the response to the Second Vatican Council, and the new pope has indicated that this will be an integral aspect of his own pontificate. John Paul the Shepherd traveled "to the ends of the earth" seeking souls for Jesus Christ, and there is little doubt that Benedict XVI will reach into the heart of old Christendom to reclaim the lost sheep in the pope's own backyard and carry them home to the Savior.

The "new era" we speak of is represented by the passing of the old and the dawning of the new millennium. The new pope stands on the threshold of that era not in the shadow of his great predecessor, but in the light of a great man, a great pope, a saint.

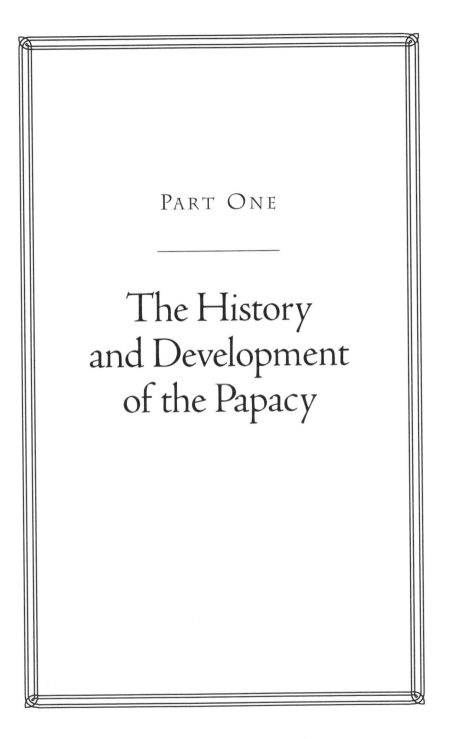

PART ONE

The History and Development of the Papacy

CHAPTER 1

"TU ES PETRUS" (CIRCA A.D. 30-1198)

T he history of the papacy, from the earliest days of the church of Rome through the rise and decline of empires, through the Renaissance, Reformation, and revolutions, is one of continual—if stop-and-start—change and evolution. The office of Bishop of Rome, the chief overseer of the church there, has developed into the primatial position in the hierarchy of the universal (one important meaning of "catholic") church. It was not always so.

The First Bishops of Rome

St. Peter the Apostle, who along with St. Paul is credited with establishing the Christian church in Rome, was an acknowledged leader among the original Twelve who were personally called and commissioned by Jesus of Nazareth. However, his role during the last twenty years of his life is not documented as well as, say, that of St. Paul, or even that of James, the brother of the Lord and an important leader of the church in Jerusalem.

During Jesus' lifetime, as recorded in the Gospels, Peter was singled out, always mentioned first in any accounting of the apostles, awarded unique powers and position among them. It is clear that Peter traveled throughout the "world" (that is, the Mediterranean region between Jerusalem and Rome) on his mission to establish and extend the Christian church. Significantly, there is no credible competing claim by any other city or nation than Rome of Peter's presence in his final days or his martyrdom. Early writers such as Clement, Ignatius, Hegesippius, Irenaeus, Tertullian, and Eusebius, among others, testify to Peter's—and Paul's—presence in the imperial capital.

In those years, from the mid–first century through the middle of the second century Anno Domini (in the year of the Lord), severe, if sporadic, imperial persecutions of the Christian churches erupted throughout the Roman Empire. The churches were forced to conduct their business underground much of the time. According to tradition, both Peter and Paul suffered martyrdom during Nero's reign, in the early 60s—in Rome itself. The office of *episkopos*, that is, bishop or overseer, had not yet been codified in Rome or anywhere else at that time.

Not until much later in the first century and the early second, as evidenced in the correspondence of Clement of Rome (circa 96) and Ignatius of Antioch (circa 107), was this ecclesiastical authority described in any detail. Was there, then, a "pope" in Rome during that first century or so after Peter's death?

It is likely that the church of Rome was governed by a *presbyterium*, that is, a council or committee of *presbyteroi*, elders or priests. These *presbyteroi*, along with the *diakonoi*—the deacons (servants)—carried out the work of teaching and social services that marked this primarily urban movement of the followers of the Jewish Messiah who had been executed under the Roman procurator of Judea, Pontius Pilate, in between A.D. 28 and 30. Such a council likely required a chairman or secretary to represent it and communicate for it; churches throughout the Mediterranean world exchanged letters and emissaries, as well as missionaries.

The names of Peter's first successors—which have survived thanks in large measure to the list published in about 180 by St. Irenaeus, the Bishop of Lyons—represent those men who probably fulfilled such ministerial functions in and for the church of Rome.

St. Pius I (circa 142–155), who appeared ninth on the list of the Bishops of Rome, can be called the first "monoepiscopal" leader (that is, a single presiding or ruling bishop) of the church of Rome. He may have been the brother of Hermas, the second-century author of the early influential Christian work known as *The Shepherd*. Pius was also the contemporary of the great theologian, Justin Martyr, and the influential heretic, Marcion.

Early Developments in the Papacy

The third century, during continued sporadic persecutions, witnessed a consolidation of the papacy's authority within the governance of the churches, especially throughout the western half of the Roman empire.

St. Victor I (189–198), the thirteenth successor of Peter, an African by birth, was the first Latin-speaking pope, which heralded an eventual change of direction and focus of the Roman church—away from the east and more "Roman" and "Italian," namely, Latin. His predecessors had been Jewish, Syrian, and Greek; subsequently, there would be fewer Greek-speakers, more Romans, and more men from prominent Roman families.

During his pontificate, Victor "picked a fight" with all the churches outside Rome, especially those in the east, who celebrated Easter at Passover itself (the fourteenth day of the Jewish month of Nisan) instead of on the Sunday *after* Passover, which was the accepted norm in Rome and the western churches. This controversy plagued the Roman church for the next few hundred years.

The first so-called antipope (that is, non-canonical pope) emerged in the early third century. St. Hippolytus, a respected presbyter and theologian, objected to the election of St. Callistus I (217–222) because he felt that Callistus, a former slave, criminal, and deacon of Pope St. Zephyrinus (198/199–217), was not doctrinally orthodox and was too lax in the discipline of the clergy. Because Hippolytus was such a strong voice in the church, he was a thorn in the side of the next two popes as well: St. Urban I (222–230) and St. Pontian (230–235). When both he and Pontian were exiled from Rome by the emperor, they reconciled and were martyred together. (Note that Hippolytus, the antipope, is also a saint.)

Subsequent popes sought to codify the government of the Roman see and further extend the authority of its bishop. Pope St. Fabian (236–250), whose election by the clergy of Rome was heralded by the appearance of a snow-white dove on his head, created seven districts within the city, each to be supervised by a deacon. This system of ecclesiastical governance (coupled with the proximity of suburban or "suburbicarian" dioceses adjacent to Rome) eventually gave birth to the college of cardinals, the chief and closest advisers to the pope—and eventually the exclusive electors of the pope.

St. Stephen I (254–257) is the first pope known to have claimed to hold the succession from Peter the Apostle, upon whom, in Matthew 16:18, the Lord laid the foundation of his *ekklesia* (assembly), or church. Thus the formal theological and historical basis of the primacy of the bishop of Rome was identified; and from that point forward, until today, some eighteen centuries later, the papacy has expanded and solidified its preeminent position in the Christian world. In Stephen's time the churches of North Africa, Alexandria, Gaul, and Spain did not recognize Rome's authority as the seat of orthodoxy and as a de facto court of appeal for doctrinal disputes (of which there were many, such as the Paschal controversy cited above).

Over the next half-century, the church faced burgeoning heresies and frequent persecutions. Finally, Emperor Constantine's edict of toleration in 313 restored status and property to the Christian churches and eventually led to official recognition of the religion by the Roman state. Constantine also convened the very first ecumenical (universal or general) council of the church, in Nicea (modern-day Turkey), in 325. The bishops of the Christian world were invited to meet in order to confront the famous heresy of Arius (that Jesus was created by God, not of the same divine substance) and confirm the doctrine of the divinity of Jesus. In all, 250 bishops participated in the council, but the bishop of Rome, St. Sylvester I (314–335) did not attend; he sent two presbyters to represent him. The next seven ecumenical councils were held in the east with little papal involvement. The First Lateran Council (1123) was called by the pope himself and held in his church, and all subsequent councils have been papal in origin.

St. Damasus I (366–384) advocated the primacy, that is, the highest rank and authority, of the papacy as "the Apostolic See." He also established Latin as the official language of the church and commissioned his secretary, St. Jerome, to write a new Latin translation of the New Testament, based on the original Greek text. The Vulgate Bible, as it became known, provided more glue to bind the western churches.

Under the reign of Emperor Theodosius the Great (379–395), Constantinople was established as the capital of the Eastern Roman

Empire. In 381, the Second Ecumenical Council recognized the bishop of Constantinople as second only to the bishop of Rome. The relationship between Rome and Constantinople would grow increasingly complicated over subsequent years, frequently due to heresies and scandals, as the Eastern church's power alternately grew and waned.

Great Popes, Troubled Times

The unity of the whole church qua Church, as opposed to the "churches" of regions and cities throughout the world, can be said to have depended upon the pope as primate, that is, as the first and chief bishop of the entire world—not just of Rome or Italy. Two of the greatest figures of late antiquity personified this aspect of the papal primacy; men who not only saved the church, but also saved Western civilization itself from complete disintegration. These popes of great spiritual and temporal power were St. Leo I (440–461) and St. Gregory I (590–604).

Leo the Great, the first of thirteen popes called Leo, was a deacon and absent from Rome on a diplomatic mission when elected as the forty-fourth successor of St. Peter. During his twenty-year pontificate he became an articulate apologist for the pope's universal authority over the churches, terming the pope "the primate of all the bishops," and exerting this authority especially in the west. His sermons and writings have survived, including the pivotal *Tome*, a letter written in 449 to Bishop Flavian of Constantinople, in which he affirmed both the divinity and the humanity of Jesus. Its teaching was affirmed by the Council of Chalcedon (451) against the heresy of Monophysitism (Christ is divine only, without a true human nature). Leo had wanted the council to be held in Italy and was represented by legates who presented his *Tome*, which was acknowledged by the council as having been spoken by "the voice of Peter."

Leo proved to be a great leader in the secular world as well. When Attila, king of the Huns, invaded Northern Italy, Leo met Attila and convinced him to spare Rome; he also convinced him to negotiate peace with the emperor. Later, when Genseric and the Vandals captured the city, Leo once again intervened and saved the city and its inhabitants.

Pope Gregory, also called "the Great" (and the only other pope besides Leo so termed, to date), the first of sixteen popes of that name, was of noble Roman lineage and had given up his civic positions to become a monk. He founded monasteries, lived an ascetic life, was made a deacon by Pope Benedict I (575–579), and embarked upon a diplomatic mission as the *apocrisiarius*, apostolic legate, to the imperial court in Constantinople. Elected unanimously upon the death of Pelagius II (579–590), Gregory was consecrated bishop of Rome under protest, thinking himself unworthy of the position. From the beginning of his pontificate he had to be concerned with the welfare of the city of Rome (his hometown) in the face of the breakdown of civil government due to the constant threat of invasion by Lombards, famine, and plague. He was an incredibly hard worker, despite frail health (damaged by his fasting regime), and faced innumerable conflicts within and without the church.

Having protected Rome from ruin, he sought better relationships with the other churches of the west, negotiated treaties that kept the invading Lombards at bay, navigated the delicate shoals of relationships with the emperor and patriarch in Constantinople (despising the Greek language and the eastern lifestyle), and sent a missionary delegation to England in 596 to resuscitate the church there. The popes who followed him were elected either because they alternatively were or were not monks—in reaction to his particular style of governance and his favoring of monks versus "diocesan" clergy. He favored the discipline of a celibate clergy and enforced rules for the election and conduct of bishops.

Pope against Emperor

Gregory I coined the term *Servus Servorum Dei* (Servant of the Servants of God) while promoting the authority of the papacy, especially in the west. For the next two hundred years much of what he built up was eroded by weak or corrupt popes—with some exceptions—who could neither govern the city of Rome nor manage the increasing demands of the imperial court in Constantinople (to approve the one elected pope, for example). Conflict, heresy, and personal immorality got in the way of smooth papal governance.

Pope Stephen III (752–757) marked a change in papal governance when, threatened yet again by the Lombards, he turned for help to the king of the Franks, Pepin III. A few years earlier, Pepin had been the recipient of a papal favor when Pope Zachary (741–752) supported Pepin's overthrow of the Merovingian dynasty, thus creating a new line from which Charlemagne would emerge. Stephen formally anointed the king near Paris and received in turn the "Donation of Pepin," a large chunk of northern and central Italy, which was the foundation of the papal state. The popes would rule this territory (which would expand and contract throughout history) for more than a thousand years, until 1870.

Leo III (795–816) crowned Pepin's son Charlemagne as the first Holy Roman Emperor on December 25, 800. These western emperors would replace the Byzantine rulers as thorns in the papal side for centuries to come.

Relations with the emperor and the patriarch in Constantinople nearly disintegrated during the reign of St. Nicholas I (858–867), due to his strict interpretation of papal authority. A particularly outstanding pope, a man of integrity, vivid personality, and vigor, he held an exalted opinion of the Petrine office with authority over bishops, synods, and all the faithful. The schismatic Photius, a layman who became the eastern patriarch, rose to prominence at this time, which exacerbated the simmering east-west church tensions; the emperor himself was upset when Nicholas excommunicated Photius.

At the turn of the second millennium of the Christian era, the pope was more or less subject to the German emperors and kings who succeeded the Frankish Charlemagne and his immediate heirs. An exception to the rule (no friend of any emperor) was Benedict IX (1032–1048). He was elected three times and deposed three times and was the third consecutive layman to assume the papal office, thanks to political upheavals in Rome and within the church hierarchy. Clement II (1046–1047) was the first pope to remain as bishop of another diocese while simultaneously bishop of Rome; he was also the first of the four "German" popes who were "nominated" (that is, imposed) by Emperor Henry III—to be followed by Damasus II (1048), St. Leo IX (1049–1054), and Victor II (1055–1057).

The East-West Schism

In 1054, the long-simmering controversies between east and west—between the patriarchates of Rome and Constantinople, in particular—boiled into open conflict over theological issues and, not incidentally, over the primacy of the Apostolic See of Rome. The leader of the church of Constantinople, the patriarch, excoriated the Latin church (the pope, in effect) for using unleavened bread in the Eucharist, eating unbled meat, suppressing the "alleluia" during Lent, enforcing clerical celibacy, and, especially, imposing the "heretical" *Filioque* clause in the creed (proclaiming that the Holy Spirit "proceeds from the Father *and* the Son," rather than from just the Father).

Leo IX delegated Cardinal Humbert de Moyenmoutier as his personal representative to the patriarch of Constantinople, Michael Cerularius, who stubbornly resisted any compromise—which resulted in bitter mutual excommunications in July 1054; Cardinal Humbert's was delivered by hand on the high altar of Santa Sophia, the greatest basilica in the east.

This breach proved to be permanent, and is known as the East-West Schism. Not until the historic meeting in 1964 when Pope Paul VI met Patriarch Athenagoras I in Jerusalem did any truly mutual move toward reconciliation occur.

Imperial Conflicts, Election Reforms

Gregory VII (1073–1085), another reforming monk in the mold of Gregory I, was a man of great intellect and religious zeal who set the papacy on a collision course with emperor and empire. He demanded and received, temporarily, the obeisance of Emperor Henry IV over the issue of lay investiture, that is, the appointment of bishops by secular rulers. He also engendered conflicts with other kings in the west, even as he initiated serious ecclesiastical reforms. He is perhaps most famous for the *Dictatus Papae*, a list of twenty-seven precepts or "dictates" of papal powers: including, "That the pope is the only one whose feet are to be kissed by all princes," "That it is legal for the pope to depose emperors," and "That the pope himself may be judged by no one."[1] The emperor drove Gregory from Rome, and the great pope died in exile and was buried in Salerno.

For four intense centuries, from the coronation of Charlemagne as Holy Roman emperor in 800 to the pontificate of Celestine III, who crowned Henry IV as Holy Roman emperor, the eighty legitimate popes were a mixed bunch who called for crusades and councils with equal fervor. Some were noblemen, others intellectuals and canon lawyers; many were elderly men, others ambitious younger politicians. At this time the college of cardinals assumed the sole responsibility for the election of the pope, as representing "the clergy and people of Rome," who were the traditional electors. Pope Nicholas II (1058–1061) decreed in 1059 that only cardinal bishops (from the dioceses adjacent to Rome) might elect the pope.

In 1179 at the Third Lateran Council, Pope Alexander III (1159–1181) decreed that a two-thirds majority of the cardinals voting was necessary to elect the pope. (Eventually, Bl. Gregory X [1272–1276] would promulgate the constitution codifying the conclave system of election, which is used to this day.) Tumultuous, disputed elections and lengthy vacancies as well as a plethora of antipopes made this era a confusing and contradictory one for those who believed in the spiritual foundation of the Petrine ministry.

CHAPTER 2

THE POPE AS RULER AND REFORMER (1198–1846)

After more than a thousand years, the papacy proved to be a durable "dynasty," an institution that survived weak popes and strong emperors. But some pontiffs seized the reins of extended temporal and military power even as they drove reforms in the church that, in many cases, are still in effect to this day.

The Vicar of Jesus Christ on Earth

Innocent III (1198–1216) stood apart from and above nearly all other popes, to say nothing of the secular rulers of his age. He was, arguably, the most powerful pope of any time, and he stood at the pinnacle of papal prestige in the high Middle Ages. The scion of a prominent noble family was elected unanimously at about age thirty-eight; he was already well known and respected as a brilliant canon lawyer and a spiritual author.

Innocent formulated a distinctly theocratic doctrine of the papacy, derived from the title that he boldly assumed, "Vicar of Jesus Christ and Successor of the Prince of the Apostles." He saw himself as "the representative of him to whom belong the earth and all that it contains and all those who inhabit it." In his "Sermon on the Consecration of a Pope" in 1198 he proclaimed that "on ascending the throne of Peter he received the power to overthrow, destroy, disperse, dispel, build, and found." This does not mean that the pope claimed to be able to destroy princes, but declared himself to be their judge: "Not only have we been placed among the princes, but since it belongs to us to judge them, we have been placed above them." Innocent saw the pope as "greater than Pharaoh" and lesser only than God himself.[1] In his spare time he declared the Magna Carta null and void—after all, King John had ceded power to the pope as England's supreme protector!

In addition to his intervention in the affairs of German emperors and English kings (in matters of divorce, episcopal appointments, and other political matters), Innocent instituted major church reforms, called the Fourth Crusade, and combated the Albigensian heresy (brutally) in France. The historic achievement of his pontificate was the Fourth Ecumenical Council of the Lateran in November 1215. This most important of medieval councils was attended by approximately twelve thousand bishops and resulted in seventy decrees on a variety of church and civil issues: including the annual reception of the sacrament of penance, the definition of "transubstantiation," the prohibition of the founding of new religious orders, and the requirement of Jews and Muslims to wear distinctive dress in public.

Boniface VIII (1295–1303) was elected on Christmas Eve 1294, when Celestine V (1294), a humble monk who had been elected against his will, abdicated after five months on the papal throne. Boniface pushed the envelope even further in his memorable militant bull, *Unam sanctum* (1302), when he proclaimed flatly, "that outside this (Catholic) church there is no salvation or remission of sins," and "that it is altogether necessary to salvation for every human creature to be subject to the

Roman pontiff."[2] Among others, the king of France was displeased and sent his soldiers to capture Boniface. The defiant pope died from exhaustion and brutal treatment at the hands of the French.

Perhaps as a reaction to the militancy of Boniface, the "Babylonian captivity" of the papacy—its years in Avignon under virtual control of France—began in 1305 and lasted for more than seventy years, through the reign of seven popes. Eventually, Pope Gregory XI (1371–1378), persuaded by the less than gentle blandishments of St. Catherine of Siena, the diminutive Dominican nun renowned for her wisdom, removed the papacy to Rome in 1377.

Schisms and Scandals

Gregory's successor, Urban VI (1378–1389), the last non-cardinal in church history to be elected pope, provoked the ecclesiastical controversy that became the greatest schism of the western church. When the new pope displayed irascible and irrational sides of his personality that the cardinals had not expected, the electors nullified their vote and chose another man, ushering in a nearly forty-year rupture in the college of cardinals and the papacy itself that resulted, from 1409 to 1417, in no less than *three* simultaneous claimants to the Throne of the Fisherman.

The Council of Constance (1414–1418) resolved the schism by deposing all three of the contemporary claimants and electing Martin V (1417–1431) at a unique conclave that included twenty-two cardinals and thirty representatives of the "five nations" (laymen and bishops from Spain, France, Italy, Germany, and England). This was the first papal conclave since 1058 and the last ever to include lay electors. Martin promised reforms, but spent his time in power reestablishing papal authority in the papal state and among the hierarchy of the church.

The Renaissance in Italy and throughout Europe brought classical knowledge, enlightenment, and an unprecedented flowering of the arts—as well as a new nadir in the papacy. Perhaps the most venal and corrupt pope ever, Alexander VI (1492–1503), a member of the notorious Spanish Borgia family, openly kept a mistress in the papal apartments; he bribed his way into office and put his family's fortunes ahead of all other considerations of church and morality.

Christianity in the New World

Spanish, Portuguese, French, and English exploration and conquest of the lands of the western hemisphere at once doubled or tripled the expanse of Christianity, bringing opportunities and headaches to the popes. A warrior pope, Julius II (1503–1513) granted to Ferdinand and Isabella of Spain, their Most Catholic Majesties and their future successors, the "right of patronage," that is, the right in perpetuity to appoint bishops and clergy to the churches in Spanish-controlled America. Throughout the next few centuries the monarchs exercised these ecclesiastical powers, setting the stage for future clashes with church authorities.

Paul III (1534–1549) authored a bull in 1537, *Sublimus Deus* (The Sublime God), which condemned mistreatment of native people in the New World, claiming their souls for Christ. He wrote:

> [We] consider, however, that the Indians are truly men and
> that they are not only capable of understanding the Catholic
> faith, but, according to our information, they desire to receive
> it. . . . [We declare] the said Indians and all other people who
> may later be discovered by Christians, are by no means to be
> deprived of their liberty or the possession of their property . . .

nor should they be in any way enslaved; should the contrary happen, it shall be null and to no effect."[3]

This was one of the first known articulations of the doctrine of anti-slavery and basic human rights in the western world.

Protestants and Jesuits

Corruption, incompetence, and perhaps political overreaching by the popes kindled the flame that erupted into the religious conflagration known as the Protestant Reformation. For years the popes retrenched or did nothing constructive in response to the critique of Martin Luther and others, until Pope Paul III (1534–1549) hesitantly convoked the Council of Trent on December 13, 1545. This council, which lasted on and off for eighteen years, touched upon virtually every major aspect of Roman Catholic doctrine: scripture and tradition, liturgy, original sin, the sacraments (especially the Eucharist), and the establishment of the seminary system for the formation of priests. All of these issues had been part of Luther's (and others') critique of the Roman church.

Pius IV (1559–1565) dissolved the Council of Trent on December 4, 1563, and subsequently confirmed its decrees, which remained the norms of the church for the next three hundred years. Under Pius, the papacy, which had been so buffeted by scandals and political turmoil, regained a measure of prestige for continuing the Tridentine reforms. The Roman Catholic Church itself entered a period of grandeur, confidence, even militancy in the face of criticism and political upheavals that would last for more than three centuries, up to the time of the First Vatican Council in 1869. Although Protestantism had gained a foothold in Europe, and would expand to North America and beyond, the Catholic church would jealously reclaim some of the spiritual and temporal authority it had lost in the Reformation (thus the term for this Tridentine period: the Counter-Reformation).

Centuries later, in 1773, Clement XIV (1769–1774) suppressed another religious congregation, the Society of Jesus (the Jesuits), after decades of charges and countercharges between the Society and European kings and clerical enemies regarding heresy and hidden agendas. Many of the popes during the sixteenth through eighteenth centuries were canon lawyers and/or diplomats; others were members of or educated in religious orders, but there had never been a Jesuit pope.

An End and a Beginning

Pope Pius VI (1775–1799) brought dusk to the long day of the old church—in effect tried to freeze it in time—and foreshadowed the modern era of the papacy, mostly through negative example. He was not a corrupt pope, but due to his personal vanity and closed mind he created more problems than he solved, leaving his successors to confront a violently new landscape in the church and in Europe (where the papacy was still focused almost exclusively). He was, arguably, the wrong man at the wrong time; he also served for a remarkably long time (the longest since Hadrian I [772–795] a thousand years earlier), though that record of longevity would be approached and surpassed by several popes over the next two hundred years.

Pius followed a relatively weak pope who was crippled by the ongoing Jesuit controversy, Clement XIV (1769–1774). He faced diplomatic and spiritual conflicts with the Prussians, the Russians (under Catherine the Great), and the revolutionary French. The Civil Constitution on the Clergy went into effect on July 12, 1790, reorganizing the French church and making the clergy salaried officials—also requiring an oath of loyalty to the regime. Pius VI dithered, but Napoleon acted; the famous general invaded the papal state in 1796, and the situation only got worse for the Roman church both in Italy and in France. Pius was deposed as head of state by the French, captured, and exiled to Florence. As Frank J. Coppa summarizes: "In 1799 Pius VI died in captivity, and the papacy seemed doomed to follow."[4]

Perhaps the most remarkable thing about the papacy in this long historical march is the very fact that it survived, that the line of succession from the so-called Prince of the Apostles, while sometimes fractured or temporarily interrupted, remained intact—and does to this day.

The Emergence of the Modern Papacy

The "modern" papacy, which dates from about the beginning of the nineteenth century, witnessed a pattern of engagement and retrenchment by various popes that has continued from 1800 to our own time, the first years of the twenty-first century after Christ.

Pope Pius VII (1800–1823) will be remembered always as the pope who was embargoed by Napoleon Bonaparte and who crowned, but did not really crown, the Corsican general and revolutionary as emperor of the French. This event, undeniable as it is, tells only part of the story—of the papacy and of Pius himself. Cardinal Luigi Barnabà Chiaramonte, a Benedictine, was elected on March 14, 1800, after a fourteen-week stalemate within the conclave at Venice. He had, as a bishop, shown independence, intelligence, and an openness to new ideas. He moved to Rome, which had been occupied by Napoleon's troops. Several years later he was arrested and held in isolation near Genoa, then transferred to Fontainbleau; there Napoleon forced the exhausted and ill pope to sign a concordat that ceded temporal and governmental powers to the emperor.

When Pius returned to Rome in 1814, he was greeted with great enthusiasm for having borne his harsh captivity with courage and resolve. He later retracted the concordat that had been executed under duress. For the next eight years he was able to focus his attention and considerable skills on governing the church and guiding it through the stormy waters of post-Napoleonic Europe. He employed a skilled secretary of state, Cardinal Ercole Consalvi, to negotiate for the Holy See at the Congress of Vienna, the international conference that reconstructed Europe after Napoleon's downfall, and which was attended by heads of state across the continent. Pius first opposed the revolutions on the South American continent, but changed his stance to neutrality, and to a limited degree favored democracy as a suitable form of government for some countries. According to papal historian J.N.D. Kelly: "[Pius] made a real attempt to adapt the papacy, within limits, to the modern world, and when he died it enjoyed a respect which it had lacked when he entered on his office; it was beginning once more to be regarded as a supra-national authority."[5]

A nobleman who had been private secretary and ambassador for Pius VI, Annibale della Genga was elected as Leo XII (1823–1829) by the votes of a conservative bloc of cardinals known as the *zelanti* (zealots). Leo represented a turn inward, away from secular political issues, toward religious and administrative concerns of the Holy See. He condemned religious toleration (tentatively smiled upon by his predecessor), reestablished the old-style feudal system in the papal state (restored to the Roman pontiff's jurisdiction by the Congress of Vienna), resurrected the Index of Forbidden Books and rejuvenated the Holy Office (formerly the Inquisition), and restricted the Jews of Rome to the ghetto and confiscated some of their properties.

Leo was unpopular in most quarters, both inside and outside the church. Of necessity, he opened a bit to the larger world, as Europe recovered from the Napoleonic wars and regained economic and political stability, and Catholic intellectuals began to engage issues such as democracy and scriptural criticism. Leo declared 1825 a Holy Year, and among his internal reforms were educational and catechetical initiatives, though he remained hostile to the modern world in nearly every act of his pontificate.

Pius VIII (1829–1830), in contrast (in a pattern that would be reenacted many times over the next two centuries), was considered a moderate-progressive when it came to doctrine and political affairs. He was Francesco Saverio Castiglione, also of noble parentage, a trained canon lawyer and a bishop since 1800. He was sixty-seven years old when elected and served for just one and one-half years as pope.

Pius instituted reforms and reversed some of the policies of Leo XII. For example, he eased the feudal-police regime in the papal state, allowed priests to assist quietly at mixed Protestant-Catholic marriages, and was active in international affairs. Pius approved the decrees of the First Plenary Council of Baltimore in the United States, which was held in 1829, and which set the still-young, still-missionary American church on its historic course of support of the papacy and fierce religious independence within American society.

During Pius VIII's pontificate the storm clouds of conflict appeared on the horizon; France swung between revolution and monarchy, Prussia gained military and political power, Austria and Spain attempted to hold onto past glories, and England remained staunchly anti-Catholic. It was a volatile mix that created concerns and crises for any man who occupied the Chair of Peter, whether he was suited to deal with them or not.

Uncompromising and backward-looking, Pius's successor, Gregory XVI (1831–1846), was the last monk to be elected pope and the last who was not a bishop. Another aristocratic scion, Bartolomeo Alberto Cappellari had been a member of a strict Benedictine order since he was eighteen, and he became "one of the church's most reactionary popes, employing Austrian troops on two occasions to crush uprisings in the papal state and opposing Italian nationalism, freedom of conscience, freedom of the press, and the separation of church and state."[6] He was the author of a 1799 work entitled *The Triumph of the Holy See and the Church against the Assaults of Innovators*.

In his defense, he immediately faced popular rebellions in the papal state and in Rome itself. Prince von Metternich, the Austrian statesman, convinced Gregory that he needed a strong secretary of state; so the pope appointed the stern-minded Cardinal Luigi Lambruschini. The cardinal supported the pope's policies denouncing states such as Portugal and Spain, whose governments flirted with pro-secular legislation. As deeply conservative and inward looking as he was, Gregory also inaugurated vigorous missionary efforts throughout the world, supported art, archaeology, and academic institutions, as well as denounced slavery as immoral and unworthy of Christians in the decree *In Supremo*. Additionally, he famously forbade the use of railroads in the papal domains, calling them *chemins d'enfer*, "roads of hell."

CHAPTER 3

THE UNIVERSAL PASTOR (1846–1978)

From the mid-nineteenth century onward, the church, and the world, changed rapidly—and radically—despite strong forces within that resisted change of any kind. Events, personalities, wars, and technology all helped the papacy rise to new heights of international visibility and influence.

The End of the Papal State

"Pio Nono," Bl. Pope Pius IX (1846–1878) reigned for nearly thirty-two years, longer than any other Roman pontiff—longer even than the undocumented traditional span credited to St. Peter (twenty-five to thirty years). Cardinal Lambruschini was runner-up in the conclave of 1847, favored by the same *zelanti*-conservative faction that had elected Leo and Gregory in previous votes. But the electors turned to a well-liked and respected moderate, Cardinal Giovanni Maria Mastai-Ferretti, the bishop of Imola. In many ways, the new pope was very different than his predecessors. He was much younger, at fifty-four, and he had traveled throughout the world, even to South America where he had served on the staff of the papal legate to Chile. The signal issues and dogmatic decrees of his pontificate fill volumes. Almost despite himself, often in response to events outside his control, Pius IX instituted the process of modernization of the papacy.

He was an immediate and almost universal hit: "a man of imposing and handsome presence who was not alarmed at the new order and as a sovereign was willing to negotiate and indeed quite anxious to make concessions to liberalism."[1] Within a month of his coronation he issued a general amnesty for political exiles and prisoners in the papal state (who numbered about two thousand from Gregory's regime), lifted restrictions on newspapers, and announced that the railway would be permitted within the papal territories! But his reign would prove arduous and controversial, and over the years Pius became much less relaxed, less liberal, and increasingly rigid in his policies.

Among his accomplishments: 1) On December 8, 1854, he defined the Immaculate Conception of the Blessed Virgin Mary—that is, he affirmed the doctrine that Mary had been born without the stain of original sin, unlike any other human being except Jesus himself. This decree sparked a renewed Marian devotion that continues to this day and is embodied by Pope John Paul II. 2) He published the encyclical *Quanta cura* (How Much Care), which included the Syllabus of Errors denouncing "the principle errors of our times," including the view that the pope might reconcile the church to "progress, liberalism, and modern civilization."[2] Thus the relation between faith and reason became a battleground within theological circles for the next century, to the deep consternation of many, on both sides. 3) Pius convoked the First Ecumenical Council of the Vatican, the first general council since Trent (1545–1563), which was historic in many regards, not the least of which was the constitution that it legislated, *Pastor aeternus* (Eternal Pastor), voted with only two in opposition on July 18, 1870. This document defined the pope's infallibility when speaking for the entire church on matters of faith and morals.

The council was suspended before it had finished its agenda when Italian troops took Rome (during the Franco-Prussian War and the war for reunification of Italy). The bishops and cardinals fled, and Pius became, famously, the self-described "prisoner of the Vatican." The papal state was lost forever, and the pope would not become a true temporal sovereign again until the Lateran Treaty of 1929.

Pius supported the theological movement called "ultramontanism," which sought to centralize authority in church government and doctrine in the Holy See, that is, in the hands of the pope and his curia. During his pontificate, jurisdiction in all such matters, including the appointment of bishops around the world, was methodically assumed by the papacy. The pope's reputation as a progressive thinker and administrator eroded over his long tenure. At the time of his death Pius IX was highly regarded by Catholics throughout the world, but exceedingly unpopular with many segments of Roman and Italian society. As Richard P. McBrien describes it: "On July 13, 1881, there was a disruption of the procession accompanying his body from its original burial place in St. Peter's to St. Lawrence's Outside the Walls. A mob tried unsuccessfully to seize the body and throw it into the Tiber River."[3]

Edging toward Modernity

What a surprise Leo XIII (1878–1903) turned out to be! Elected at age sixty-eight, the frail-appearing Cardinal Gioacchino Vincenzo Pecci was expected to be a caretaker pope who would serve a short time (in contrast to Pius's extraordinarily lengthy reign). Cardinal Pecci had been opposed and kept away from the seat of power by Cardinal Giacomo

Antonelli, Pius IX's powerful secretary of state (a layman), but brought to Rome as camerlengo, or papal chamberlain, after Antonelli's death, thus presiding at the conclave that elected him to keep the chair warm for a longer-term successor.

Twenty-five years later the ninety-three-year-old pontiff died after a remarkably fruitful pontificate, which spanned the nineteenth and twentieth centuries. He is considered the first truly modern pope; Pius IX had been the first "media pope," in a time when communication, transportation, photography, and other technologies began to explode and papal images such as "holy cards" and statuettes were widely distributed throughout the world. Leo experienced the same phenomenon, but in contrast to Pius, he became more popular as time went on, rather than less so. Leo very consciously attempted to point the church in a new direction vis-à-vis the modern world. However, according to J.N.D. Kelly, "far from halting centralization, as progressives hoped, he increased it by intervening with national episcopates, strengthening the position of nuncios [the pope's ambassadors], and concentrating orders and congregations in Rome."[4]

Leo's greatest achievement is almost universally deemed to be the historic encyclical, *Rerum novarum* (Of New Things), promulgated on May 15, 1891, which advocated just wages, workers' rights, trade unions, respect for work and workers, and social justice. This document had—and still has—profound effects on Catholic theology and social action, especially regarding the dignity of the human person and his relationship to his family, society, and government.

In foreign policy, Leo XIII had his hands full, and he focused on the attempt to recover the papal state. He confronted the German anti-clerical laws (known by the catch-term *Kulturkampf*), mediated disputes among the European powers, and established nearly two hundred fifty new dioceses throughout the world. Regarding the American Catholic Church, in 1892 the pontiff appointed the first apostolic delegate to the United States and in 1899 condemned "Americanism," a movement in the U.S. that sought to adapt Catholicism to contemporary needs.

The Retreat from Modernism

The 1903 conclave, the first of the twentieth century, saw the election of Giuseppe Melchiorre Sarto, the son of a postmaster, a renowned pastor and bishop, most recently the patriarch of Venice, at age sixty-eight. For the last time in history the *jus exclusivae* (right of exclusion) was used by Austria to veto Cardinal Rampolla, who was the front-runner in the election to that point.

Pope St. Pius X (1903–1914), the last pope to date to be canonized a saint, adopted as his motto: "To restore all things in Christ" (from Ephesians 1:10). Although his natural inclinations were spiritual and pastoral, inevitably, he was drawn into the political disputes and controversies of his time, in Italy and elsewhere. Pius's secretary of state, Cardinal Rafael Merry del Val, a deeply conservative Spaniard, advised on and executed the pope's policies regarding foreign governments, showing a distinct disdain for democracies and the separation of church and state.

Pius's encyclical *Lamentabili sane* (Lamentably Departed) of July 3, 1907, strongly condemned sixty-five modernist propositions, including those that concerned divine revelation, biblical studies, and the divinity of Jesus—part of Pius's ongoing war on the heresy of modernism. He reorganized the Roman Curia, streamlining the organization of the papal administrative offices, and commissioning a revision of canon law. Furthermore, he reformed seminaries and catechetical instruction, including the preparation of a new catechism, and stimulated Catholic spirituality through urging frequent (even daily, which was startling at the time) reception of Holy Communion and other liturgical reforms.

Pius died on the eve of World War I. He had been a magnetic presence, a strong, conservative (critics said reactionary) Holy Father who exuded piety and humility. He was canonized forty years after his death.

In a World at War

Mass devastation, reminiscent of the last days of the Roman Empire, spread across Europe and the world in the twentieth century. This created new burdens for the popes as spokesmen for peace, and mass communications gave them the pulpit from which to preach.

Benedict XV (1914–1922), born Giacomo Della Chiesa, was a scholar and diplomat. He had been secretary to Leo XIII's secretary of state, Cardinal Rampolla, and thus earned the enmity of Pius XI's secretary of state, Cardinal Merry del Val, who persuaded Pius to "banish" Della Chiesa from the diplomatic corps to Bologna as archbishop (withholding the red hat for seven years). Benedict was crowned in the Sistine Chapel at the relatively young age of sixty.

World War I preoccupied the pope's time. The war was a mixed blessing for him, because he showed firm moral authority and began to attract diplomatic representatives to the Holy See in this time of crisis: by the end of his reign, twenty-seven countries, including Great Britain, had ambassadors assigned to the court of the pope, who held moral sway over hundreds of millions of people throughout the world. However, Benedict was excluded from post-war negotiations. He hoped for and worked for reunion with the schismatic eastern Orthodox churches, and he promoted missionary activities and the ordination of native clergy among mission countries. His death from influenza, after seven years, was unexpected and widely mourned.

Achille Ratti held three doctorates and was a librarian as well as a diplomat, landing as cardinal-archbishop of Milan in 1921. He took the name Pius XI (1922–1939) upon his election at age sixty-five. This Pius was an energetic pontiff who attempted to ease the tensions of the previous thirty years regarding modernism; he rehabilitated some of the theologians who had been banned in Pius X's time. He was open to scientific and biblical research, called for reunion between the Latin and Orthodox churches, and supported workers' activism in the vein of Leo XIII's promptings in *Rerum novarum*.

As had been and ever would be the case for the Supreme Pontiff, he became entangled in politics and foreign relations. Pius deftly negotiated the Lateran Treaty with Mussolini's Italian government in 1929, creating the Vatican City State as it exists today. For the first time since 1879, the pope was a temporal sovereign of a recognized state. He favored Generalissimo Francisco Franco in the bloody Spanish civil war, gradually hardened his stance against fascism, bitterly opposed the Bolshevik communists who had seized power in Russia—and entered into a concordat with Nazi Germany to protect the rights of Catholics in that vicious totalitarian state.

Pius supported historical preservation in the Vatican collections. He created Vatican Radio in 1931 and became the first pope to use the medium. He was a tough, even harsh administrator, not a collaborative leader (he downplayed the role of the college of cardinals throughout his pontificate). Despite the ominous clouds of war on the European horizon, he tilted toward the Italian and German governments against the hated Soviets, but broke off the concordat with the Nazis in 1937 when it became clear to him that the church would not be respected under Hitler. He also laid the groundwork for the renewal movement within the church that would culminate in the Second Vatican Council two decades after his death.

Pius XII (1939–1958) was the last aristocrat, to date, to occupy the papal throne, and his pontificate reflected his background as well as his immense intellectual gifts. As his predecessor's secretary of state, Eugenio Pacelli was equipped as no other cardinal to carry the burdens of the papacy in a time of total war in Europe and around the world. In fact, he served for most of his pontificate as his own secretary of state, a remarkable break in tradition that also somewhat devalued the role of that position in subsequent pontificates. He was elected on the first day of the conclave.

Before, during, and after World War II, Pope Pius urged peace, prayed for peace, and worked for peace. He attempted to be a pastor as well as a diplomat as the world exploded into conflict all around him. The Germans occupied Rome, but the Holy Father made Vatican City, the tiny state founded on the presumed burial site of St. Peter, an asylum and sanctuary for refugees, including many Jews.

Pius has been criticized by a number of historians and others for failing to speak out more forcefully and clearly on behalf of the Jews who were persecuted in the Holocaust throughout the war years. McBrien offers this analysis: "Those who have written in defense of his wartime posture underscore his denunciation of the extermination of peoples based on race, albeit in general terms, his concern that stronger and more explicit denunciations would lead to even greater reprisals [against Catholics and Jews], and his personal support for efforts to render assistance and refuge to Jews."[5] The controversy will continue.

Catholic and Jewish historians have sought access to the archival materials in the Vatican to look at the primary documents of the period. Other documents and memoirs support the contention that Pius helped save some thousands of Jewish lives. However, in contrast to Pius XI's strong position of opposition to the Nazi regime in 1937, Pius XII's carefully nuanced response appears tepid to critics sixty years later.

Pius was a highly disciplined and productive administrator, producing encyclicals that covered a vast range of Catholic concerns. He defined the doctrine of the Assumption of the Blessed Virgin Mary on November 1, 1950 (the first and only infallible declaration of a pope since the First Vatican Council's controversial definition) and declared a Holy Marian Year in 1954. Pius canonized a total of thirty-three new saints, a large number in its time (subsequently dwarfed by John Paul II's activity). And he increased the size and scope of the college of cardinals, something his successors continued to do; he reduced the Italian contingent to about one-third of the total membership of the sacred college. Pius XII vastly increased the visibility of the papacy through his judicious use of mass media, firmly placing the Petrine office within the consciousness of the entire world during his lengthy pontificate.

The Second Vatican Council

Cardinal Giuseppi Roncalli's peasant stock recalled that of Pius X, and the patriarch of Venice, who had been a teacher, pastor, and diplomat for forty years was an attractive, friendly face for the papacy, a stark contrast to the austere Pius XII. Bl. John XXIII (1958–1963) was elected a month shy of his seventy-seventh birthday as a presumed "caretaker" pope as Leo XIII had been in 1878—and, like Leo, he stunned the world. In 1959, Pope John called for a new ecumenical council, the first in ninety years, to resolve once and for all the issue of the church's relation to the world and to update the language and presentation of its ancient teachings—all while preserving the deposit of faith that had been passed down by the apostles. The most visible changes would be liturgical, the celebration of mass in local languages and the reception of Holy Communion under both species (wafer and wine).

This *aggiornamento* (updating) caused deep rippling effects and resentments among many Catholics—including some members of the hierarchy—that are felt within the church some forty years later. But few doubt the sincerity and holiness of this peasant-born pontiff who burned so brightly, like a shooting star across the sky of history in the dark time of Cold War that almost ignited in nuclear war.

John's major encyclicals included *Mater et magistra* (Mother and Teacher), May 15, 1961, which was a statement on Catholic social teaching. His *Pacem in terris* (Peace on Earth), April 11, 1963, was a strong statement—addressed not just to Catholics, but also to all mankind—on human rights and human responsibility, calling for dialogue between the communist east and the capitalist west. He also devoted attention to the reconciliation between and among the Christian churches, a preoccupation of nearly all the modern popes.

After he convened the first session of Vatican II (October–December 1962), it became clear that his health was failing. He died of stomach cancer on June 3, 1963. The whole world mourned. He was beatified in 2001, but is already considered a true saint by many millions.

Paul VI's pontificate (1963-1978) is a "perfect" one to study and reflect upon: fifteen years in length, encompassing the later years of the Second Vatican Council, filled with theological and doctrinal issues as well as a volatile world situation, and imbued with his unique personality. The last few years were especially rife with controversy and personal difficulties for this man who was supremely suited to be pope by training and intellectual ability, but stymied by his drive to compromise and find common ground among warring parties within the post-conciliar Roman Catholic Church.

The man, Giovanni Batista Montini, was, like Pius XII, a near-perfect *papabile*, with just the right blend of scholarly, diplomatic, political, bureaucratic, and pastoral experience. He had been a progressive force at the council and a bridge builder between the liberal and conservative factions, trying (often successfully) to bring them together during the first session. He could have suspended or canceled the council, but he did not, thus taking upon himself the mantle of his predecessor and making the council his own.

Paul VI will be remembered primarily for his July 25, 1968, encyclical, *Humanae vitae* (Of Human Life), in which the pope reaffirmed the church's teachings on marriage and reproduction, and against any form of artificial birth control. In the liberal western countries, such as the United States, the teaching was received as a bitter and surprising pill, because a special commission appointed by the pope himself had advised him to reconsider the traditional teaching in light of contemporary theological and scientific understanding.

His other documents and proclamations regarding ecumenism, the Catholic priesthood, the "real presence" of Christ in the Eucharist, the economic gap between rich and poor, liturgical reform, and missionary evangelization were a blend of orthodoxy, liberalism, and compromise. He was personally shaken by violence in the world, including the assassination of the former Italian prime minister and friend, Aldo Moro in 1978 and an attempt on his own life in Manila in 1975. He also enlarged the sacred college of cardinals and set a cap on the age of cardinal-electors of the pope at eighty.

Pope Paul became increasingly frail and mystical in his final years. There was talk of his possible retirement, especially after he required other bishops to submit their resignations at age seventy-five. But he soldiered on dutifully, if sadly until he died of a heart attack on August 6, 1978, at Castelgandalfo, the pope's summer residence outside Rome. His death ushered in the "year of three popes." He was genuinely mourned as a profoundly faithful man of God.

A Short-Lived Pontificate

For thirty-three days the world watched John Paul I (August–September 1978) with fascination. Here was a new kind of pope: friendly, humorous, humble, the complete pastor. Albino Luciani had been content to be the patriarch of Venice (the third one in the twentieth century to be elected pope, after Pius X and John XIII). What happened? Although there was no autopsy after his death (the precedent having been established by order of Pius X in 1914), it is now clear that he was ill upon his election and the severe strain and lack of proper medical care spelled his doom.

He was not murdered, despite conspiracy theories (which doesn't negate the dark rumors of financial shenanigans in the Vatican Bank and the upper echelons of Italian business and banking), nor was he piously reading *The Imitation of Christ*, nor was he discovered by his priest-secretary; the Vatican botched the announcement with fibs and unnecessary cover-up of the circumstances, namely, that a nun (a female!) had found the dead pope, rather than a male celibate priest. John Paul had been liked, even beloved, during his short pontificate, and he set the stage for the next chapter of history that few, if any, could foresee.

CHAPTER 4

POPE JOHN PAUL II
(1978–2005)

History is rarely a neat process. Our efforts to tidy up or package the chronicles of great lives and momentous events most often end in at least partial failure. Yet sometimes, despite human folly, a seemingly divine order may be discerned in the life of a great historical figure. Such is the case of Pope John Paul II, who reigned as Supreme Pontiff of the Roman Catholic Church from his election on October 16, 1978, until his death on April 2, 2005. He was a historical person of the first magnitude, one who will be written about for centuries to come: debated, admired, criticized, inscribed in the pantheon of world figures and in the catalogue of the saints. He has been pope longer than all but one other on historical record, and his legacy as a religious leader can be compared to the apostles of the time of Christ from whom he derived his commission to teach, to heal, and to feed the souls of all nations.

For John Paul, St. Peter was no mere predecessor of long ago, but a living presence, as were the thirteen score other men who had occupied Peter's Chair. It is easy to imagine that John Paul would have been an important and influential bishop of Rome in whatever era he had lived, whether in the earliest centuries in the face of persecution and heresy, the Middle Ages or Age of Revolutions, even the nineteenth century leading to the First Vatican Council. It is possible to say this with some assurance because he seemed to embody the entire history of the church in his being.

From his tragic, war-torn youth to his formation as a priest in Poland, from his parochial and academic assignments to his episcopacy at a young age (auxiliary bishop at thirty-eight, archbishop at forty-three, cardinal at forty-seven) under the communist regime in Poland—and ultimately to his surprise election as pope in the chilliest days of the Cold War—Karol Wojtyla was, it can now be said, born to be pope.

Early Days

He was born on May 18, 1920, in Wadowice, Poland, the second son of a pensioned army lieutenant, for whom he was named, and a mother, Emilia, who died when he was a small child. His elder brother Edmund died at age twenty-six of scarlet fever when Karol was twelve. He displayed intellectual and athletic gifts in his school years, moving to Krakow to enter the Jagellonian University, a state institution, in 1938. The German invasion of Poland interrupted his studies, though he continued to write and to act with clandestine groups. When he was twenty, he was made a laborer at a German-controlled limestone quarry and a year later at a chemical plant. At twenty-two, he became an underground seminarian, as theological studies were banned, and he was ordained after the end of World War II on November 1, 1946. Following further studies in Rome, where he received his doctorate in 1948, he assumed his first parish assignment.

In 1958, Pope Pius XII appointed Karol Wojtyla auxiliary bishop of Krakow. Then on December 30, 1963, after serving as the temporary administrator to the archdiocese of Krakow and participating in the first two sessions of the Second Vatican Council, he was named archbishop. He was a recognized pastoral and intellectual presence among the participants in the council. On June 28, 1967, Pope Paul VI created Wojtyla a cardinal.

Throughout this period, in the twenty-five years before his election as pope, Wojtyla published widely: poetry, books, drama, philosophy, theology. His reputation as a thinker spread throughout Catholic academic circles across the globe. Significantly, he was chosen to preach the annual Curial Lenten retreat in Rome in March 1976, with the aging Paul VI in attendance; he toured the United States in the summer of 1976.

Election as Pope

Nearly everyone in the church, even the savviest of Vatican insiders, was surprised by the election of Karol Wojtyla, the archbishop of Krakow, as Pope John Paul II on October 16, 1978. At age fifty-eight, he was young for the job (Pius IX had been fifty-four, but the average age over the previous two hundred years was sixty-three), which promised a lengthy pontificate. He was healthy and vigorous, in contrast to his immediate predecessors who had been frail men. He was the first non-Italian pope in 455 years, since the Englishman Hadrian VI (1522–1523), which in itself was thought to be—indeed proved to be—a momentous change in direction for the papacy.

John Paul's Polish roots were always evident during his pontificate, as seen through his Polish religiosity, manifested by a staunch devotion to the Blessed Virgin Mary and by a prayer life of immense depth and scope. Mary is the single most powerful symbol of Polish culture and nationhood. Poland has been for a thousand years, and remains today, even as it experiences a time of increased secularization, the most overwhelmingly Catholic country in the world. John Paul II was, from the moment of his election, "the Polish Pope."

John Paul II traveled more than any pope in history, canonized more saints than any pope in history, spoke more languages (seventeen), and wrote more books, encyclicals, constitutions and apostolic letters combined than any pope in history. In fact, there have been few popes like him in all of history. It is possible that he will be remembered as "John Paul the Great," a superlative given to only two others, and those in the first millennium of the church. Why? Biographer George Weigel puts it succinctly and directly:

> If the church of the future knows John Paul II as "John Paul
> the Great" it will be for this reason: at another moment of
> peril, when barbarisms of various sorts threatened civiliza-
> tion, a heroic figure was called from the church to meet the
> barbarian threat and propose an alternative. In the case of
> Leo the Great (440–461), the barbarians in question were Attila
> and his Huns. In the case of Gregory the Great (590–604), the
> barbarians were the Lombards. In the case of John Paul II,
> the barbarism threatening civilization has been a set of ideas
> whose consequences include barbarous politics—defective
> humanisms that, in the name of humanity and its destiny,
> create new tyrannies and compound human suffering.[1]

At his election, John Paul II committed himself to fulfill the Second Vatican Council. With his first encyclical, *Redemptor hominis* (Redeemer of Mankind), published on March 4, 1979, he focused on the social teaching of the council and his own personal experiences in the fight for human dignity and justice under communist rule. He continued to issue such documents throughout his papacy on spiritual, ecclesiastical, and moral matters. In 1991 alone he published two key documents: *Redemptoris missio* (The Mission of the Redeemer) and *Centesimus annus* (The Hundredth Year), in explicit commemoration of Leo's *Rerum novarum*, in support of workers' rights and the dignity of all human work. In addition, his homilies and pastoral letters that coincided with his extensive world travels nearly always had a sharp theological edge—not surprising from this agile philosopher and engaged pastor.

On a practical political and bureaucratic level, John Paul had a tremendous impact on church governance by the simple fact of his longevity, which allowed him to appoint more bishops and cardinals than nearly any other pope (a total of 232 in nine consistories, the last of which was October 21, 2003). In a pontificate of more than a quarter-century, there were innumerable points of high achievement and crisis, historic accomplishments both theological and political, as well as a return to personal piety and Marian devotion that is simply remarkable in a post-modern and post-Vatican II church.[2]

Achievements and Controversies

Some of the important facets of this historic pontificate are outlined below:

First, he survived—barely—the assassination attempt in St. Peter's Square on May 13, 1981. But more than his physical survival, which he attributed to the intercession of the Mother of Christ, his patroness, the aftermath of the attempt revealed links between the assassin and the Eastern European security apparatus, possibly even the Soviet KGB. John Paul's political and spiritual opposition to communism, contributing to its downfall in his own country and throughout Europe, had hit a nerve. He continued the struggle throughout the 1980s, including support of the Polish Solidarity resistance movement. He personally negotiated with Soviet leader Mikhail Gorbachev to gain religious freedoms for Christians, Jews, and Muslims within the communist sphere. He stood as a rock against which the storms of political opposition crashed and died. The moral authority of the papacy reached a new apex during this time as an essentially non-violent moral revolution succeeded. He reasserted the papacy's pivotal position in world affairs in a way not seen since Innocent III.

Second, in his travels to countries friendly and unfriendly to the church (129 foreign countries on 104 international journeys), Pope John Paul II maintained a consistent message to the people, based on a fundamentally orthodox Christian theology laced with deep personal mysticism. He criticized the excesses of capitalism along with the repressions of communist and other tyrannical regimes. Ultimately, his critique of Marxism throughout the world was spectacularly successful, in that communism ended in many countries, just as he predicted. The other side of the same coin saw the pope's opposition to liberation theology when that movement embraced violent resistance as a part of its teaching. John Paul spoke primarily, but not exclusively, to Catholic audiences; he commanded a world stage from the beginning of his pontificate, and he never left it during his lifetime.

Thirdly, this pope changed the office of the papacy in its style and substance in ways that harken back to some of the greatest figures in church history, such as St. Gregory I, Gregory VII, or Innocent III. As a trained actor and an experienced archbishop, John Paul knew how to engage an audience like few public figures of our time, or any other.

His more than one hundred foreign trips and thousand weekly general audiences brought him out to meet face-to-face with hundreds of millions of people, making him the most seen celebrity in all of history. Youth especially were drawn to him, even in his old age, when he traveled to Manila, Denver, Toronto, and Paris to celebrate his special connection with the young. Presidents, tyrants, and kings came and went during his pontificate, but John Paul outlived most of them.

A fourth major aspect of John Paul's pontificate is his continuity with and fulfillment of the Second Ecumenical Council of the Vatican. He was the first pope fully "of" the council, and he will be the last who was a council father. As a young bishop from Krakow, Karol Wojtyla played an active role in the council, winning a reputation for erudition and spirituality. Although he deferred always to his senior, the Primate of Poland, Cardinal Stefan Wyszynski, he spoke and wrote eloquently about the agenda items that the council confronted.

He was already well-known in Poland for his groundbreaking book on sex and marriage titled *Love and Responsibility* (published in 1960), which was a startlingly frank discussion of the topics that so many Catholics (priests and lay people) simply didn't or couldn't talk about. After the council, in his home diocese, he enthusiastically implemented the liturgical changes of the council as a committed shepherd among an energized flock, and his reputation flourished.

As pope, he consciously—and cautiously—carried out the agenda of the Second Vatican Council, though in this regard he met the critics, again. His prefect of the Congregation for the Doctrine of the Faith (which used to be, at various times throughout history, the Inquisition, then the Holy Office) from 1981 onward was Cardinal Joseph Ratzinger of Germany (who had been a *peritus*, a theological adviser). Ratzinger, a brilliant theologian, became known as a fierce watchdog of orthodoxy, with the power to make—or break—any Catholic thinker who put his or her head above the trench line. On balance, John Paul's was a distinctly conservative, go-slow approach to the many initiatives that came out of Vatican II.

Fifth, much of his time as bishop of Rome was spent addressing the issues that separate branches of the Christian faith and non-Christian religions from one another. He placed great importance on the relationships among the "separated brethren," or other Christian churches—especially the Orthodox churches of the east. Since Vatican II opened the door to dialogue and common prayer, this pope took advantage of every opportunity to meet with and pray with Christian leaders from around the world. As noted earlier, his invitation to them to join in a dialogue about the primacy of "Peter" was in itself a remarkably open step toward possible, eventual reconciliation.

On one issue, however, John Paul differed from several other Christian churches. One of his most controversial statements appeared in the apostolic letter of May 22, 1994, *Ordinatio sacerdotalis* (On the Reserving of Priestly Ordination to Men Alone), in which he closed any discussion of the possibility of the ordination of women as priests. He cited scriptural and papal teachings as prohibiting the practice that has been adopted (not without controversy) by the Anglican communion and other Christian denominations. He stated flatly that women are incapable of receiving holy orders in this way.

Crucially, Pope John Paul also spent considerable energy on repairing and renewing the relations between Catholics and Jews. Having grown up with Jewish friends and being, even as a child on the soccer fields of Wadowice, an outspoken opponent of anti-Semitism, John Paul brought special empathy to his role as conciliator and brother among the children of Abraham. One of his very first visits as pope was to the main synagogue of Rome. He visited the Holocaust Museum in Israel in 2001 and delivered a moving address on the tragic crime against humanity that was the Shoah. He prayed at the Wailing Wall in Jerusalem. To Jews, Protestant Christians, Muslims, and all non-Catholics, John Paul II apologized prayerfully and profusely, asking forgiveness for the sins that the "sons and daughters" of the Catholic Church had committed against them throughout history.

Death and Legacy

The life and pontificate of John Paul II began to draw to an end on Thursday, March 31, 2005. Across the globe, billions kept vigil around the clock via news coverage on all major media outlets. In St. Peter's Square, the site of so much of the church's history over the past five centuries, immense crowds swelled during daylight and ebbed somewhat in the later hours, only to grow in size and intensity of expectation when the sun rose again. The images broadcast to every continent were those of men and women of all ages and races and religions. The Catholic faithful, 1.1 billion in number, gathered for prayer in homes, churches, and public meeting places everywhere—especially in the pope's native Poland, with the most fervent family feelings in Krakow, where he had been a priest and bishop before he had been pope.

Sorrow—and, for many, relief that his suffering had finally ended—prevailed when on the evening of Saturday, April 2, the official announcement came from the Vatican: at 9:30 p.m. (Rome time) the Holy Father had passed from earthly life into eternity. Among those hundreds of thousands who had gathered in the piazza before the lighted windows of his private apartment in the Apostolic Palace, there was no doubt that the eighty-four-year-old Roman pontiff was a saint in heaven. After a final, painful public appearance on March 30, having survived Easter 2005, he had died of infection, septic shock, and failure of multiple major organs.

The city of Rome greeted, then groaned under the overwhelming weight of millions of pilgrims who rushed to the Apostolic See, the church founded by St. Peter and St. Paul according to hoary tradition. Again, cameras and microphones recorded the sight. It was an unprecedented event. This pilgrim-apostle, who tirelessly reached out to the very ends of the earth with the Gospel message in answer to his commission from Christ to preach to all nations, now drew them to himself in death.

Almost stealthily, the cardinals of the Catholic Church who are residential archbishops outside of Rome booked flights and departed their dioceses—as far-flung as Bombay and Buenos Aires, Khartoum and Krakow, Los Angeles and Lviv—for the ancient city where the pontiff would be laid to rest, and where they would, in little more than two weeks, gather in conclave to elect his successor.

John Paul II had taken center stage in the global drama from the moment he had been announced in St. Peter's Square in 1978. Even though the world had watched his agonizing physical decline over nearly a decade, his loss still was still difficult to accept. He had not taken an unaided step in two years—in fact he had been confined to a mini-throne that could be maneuvered easily through the chambers of the Vatican and in the grand sanctuary of St. Peter's Basilica—yet he had insistently and stubbornly kept to a grueling schedule filled with public audiences, public masses, and consistories, as well as greeting fellow heads of state and ambassadors, and meeting with curial officials. It was deemed a miracle by some that he had lived to observe his silver jubilee as pope on October 16, 2003—even creating thirty new cardinals within the following week.

With a Slavic constitution of iron and by dint of sheer will and faith in God, John Paul II had not only outlived many of those touted as likely future popes, but he had confounded friends and critics alike by remaining lucid and commanding, filled with a joyful spirit despite his suffering. Most importantly, he had retained the prayerful humility (despite formidable intellectual gifts) that had attracted his fellow cardinals to vote for him in the conclave when he had been only fifty-eight years old, the bold choice that had surprised the world.

Even he had understood, though he spoke infrequently about it in public, the price and peril of his illnesses. During the long twilight of his pontificate there were calls, both aloud and whispered, for his resignation. What if he had fallen into an irreversible coma or had been paralyzed, or unable to speak? It was known that he had left instructions for such contingencies, but nowhere in canon law or papal tradition are there any provisions for putting aside a pope—for whatever reason, legitimate or not.

Papal resignations have been rare, voluntary papal resignations even rarer. Death is the only end for a pope, unless he wishes to break precedent and change a fundamental aspect of the Petrine ministry—which John Paul II considered, according to his testament, but eschewed.

On Good Friday (March 25), the Holy Father had not attended the Stations of the Cross in the Coliseum—one of the Holy Week observances that he missed for the first time in his pontificate. Cardinal Joseph Ratzinger, the prefect of the Congregation for the Doctrine of the Faith and dean of the college of cardinals, wrote and delivered the meditations on the Passion of Christ, standing in for his aged friend, the pope. Cardinal Ratzinger wrote, movingly and prophetically, about the seventh station ("Jesus falls for the second time"):

> Lord Jesus Christ, you have borne all our burdens and you continue to carry us. Our weight has made you fall. Lift us up, for by ourselves we cannot rise from the dust.... Keep us sober and vigilant, capable of resisting the forces of evil. Help us to recognize the spiritual and material needs of others, and to give them the help they need. Lift us up, so that we may lift others up. Give us hope at every moment of darkness, so that we may bring your hope to the world.[3]

The ailing pope watched and listened on closed-circuit TV in his private chapel, with his back turned to a camera trained on him. Then, he was unable to preside at mass on Easter Sunday. Each time a picture was taken during the final two weeks, he seemed more frail, more distant, more ill. Yet the Christian world, engaged in the annual celebration of the resurrection of Jesus Christ—the great alleluia of the liturgical calendar—seemed finally to accept the fact that the Bishop of Rome, the Successor of St. Peter, simply could not manage the physical requirements of public ceremonies. The final difficult Wednesday wave and blessing, three days before his death, said it all.

Suddenly, the streams of mourners, estimated at more than two million, stood in line for uncounted hours to file past the body as it lay in state in the basilica. In his final public appearance, as an unmistakable sign of his deep humility, John Paul II wore brown walking shoes instead of the traditional red slippers, which contrasted dramatically with the formal vestments—red chasuble, white miter, and shepherd's staff (crosier)—in which his body was dressed. He seemed almost two-dimensional as he lay upon the bier amid a constant flow of mourners, including the heads of state and church officials, many of whom arrived the day before the funeral rites.

A mass of Christian burial, with pontifical elements, was celebrated by Cardinal Ratzinger—soon to be elected pope himself—and con-celebrated by the college of cardinals. The funeral was unprecedented in size and was attended by—in addition to the bishops of Italy and diplomatic delegations—world leaders including the presidents of France and Iran, King Juan Carlos of Spain, and, for the first time, the president of the United States. The piazza was filled to capacity with about 200,000 people, and more than a million other pilgrims spilled out along the Via della Conciliazione and into side streets all the way to the Tiber River.

The world leaders and mourners present, a television audience of billions, and the college of cardinals heard Ratzinger's preaching loudly and clearly:

> "Follow me." The Risen Lord says these words to Peter. They
> are his last words to this disciple, chosen to shepherd his
> flock. "Follow me"—this lapidary saying of Christ can be
> taken as the key to understanding the message which comes to
> us from the life of our late beloved Pope John Paul II. Today
> we bury his remains in the earth as a seed of immortality—
> our hearts are full of sadness, yet at the same time of joyful
> hope and profound gratitude . . . .[4]

Cardinal Ratzinger recalled the life story of Karol Wojtyla, whom he had met at the Second Vatican Council in Rome in the early 1960s when both were much younger: the German, a *peritus* (theological adviser), and the Pole, an auxiliary bishop of the Archdiocese of Krakow. The seventy-seven-year-old cardinal, whose next birthday would be marked before the beginning of the conclave, April 16, spoke with energy and conviction, tinged with humility and sorrow at such a great personal loss.

John Paul remained a very real presence for Ratzinger as he eulogized the man who had loomed so large over the church and the world. The two had "grown up" as theologians after the council, throughout the '60s and '70s. Wojtyla became archbishop of his diocese and a cardinal in 1967. Ratzinger had been appointed Archbishop of Munich and Freising in 1977, elevated to the cardinalate by Pope Paul VI just three months later. The two men were fellow cardinals for less than a year and one-half before Wojtyla was elected in the surprising second conclave of 1978.

Finally, the dean of the college of cardinals, the close confidant, theological mentor, and adviser of the late pope offered these words: "None of us can ever forget how in that last Easter Sunday of his life, the Holy Father, marked by suffering, came once more to the window of the Apostolic Palace and one last time gave his blessing *urbi et orbi*. We can be sure that our beloved pope is standing today at the window of the Father's house, that he sees us and blesses us."

The tomb of John Paul II, in the grotto of the popes beneath the main altar of the basilica where he had celebrated so many liturgies, lay open to the public within a few days of his death. The pilgrims continued to stream in to pray for—and to—their sainted shepherd.

To all who spoke about him, to all who mourned him, to all who had known him or even seen him once from a distance, Pope John Paul

II had been—and would always remain—one of the most powerful and prophetic examples of true Christian living.

For John Paul II, the human encounter with God was the central event and purpose of human life. He believed with all his soul that the revelation of God's love is to be found in the life, death, and resurrection of Jesus Christ. This was evident throughout his life, from his student thesis on St. John of the Cross through his last years on the papal throne, much of which was spent in deep prayer and direct communion with his Lord. Despite his profound understanding of the twentieth century as one of hopelessness and fear for so many ("Be not afraid," he counseled from his very first days as pope), and despite his own horrific experiences in World War II and under the communist regime in Poland, he experienced the presence of God in a very real and immediate way. Similarly, he experienced the presence and support of Mary, the Mother of God.

John Paul sought to bring light into the darkness of our age; hope and faith into our despairing hearts. Did he accomplish this mission? Or must he be deemed less than a success, given the deplorable state of the world and the misery of billions of its inhabitants, Christians and non-Christians alike? This man of many faces and talents—actor, pastor, teacher, leader, writer, mystic, philosopher, witness—will be remembered for his intelligent and vigorous exercise of papal authority and the increasing centralization of power in the Vatican. As pontiff and Supreme Pastor, he was truly a bridge-builder between the human and the divine.

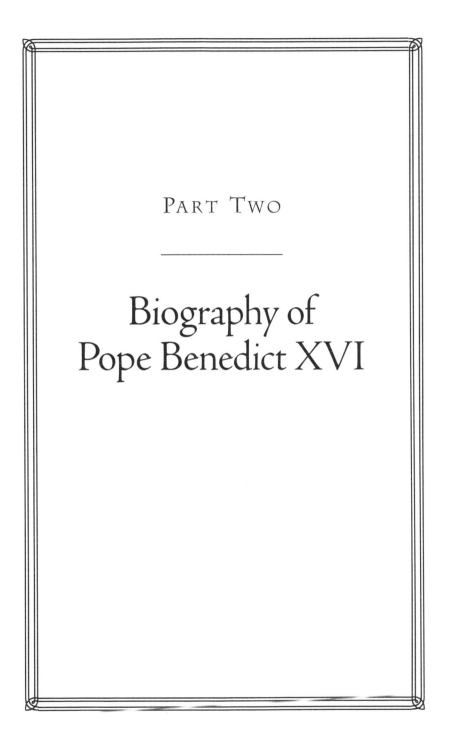

PART TWO

Biography of
Pope Benedict XVI

CHAPTER 5

THE CONCLAVE

The inside story of the conclave of 2005 began to seep out, like smoke, almost immediately. It was one of the shortest in history, compared to the two-day conclave in 1963 at the election of Paul VI and one-day conclave of 1978, which elected John Paul I. At first-blush, it appeared that the cardinals had already made up their minds before entering the sealed-off Sistine Chapel. This proved not to be the case. However, it is clear that ten days of pre-conclave preparation and several years of behind-the-scenes reflection (and perhaps some politicking) helped to move the voting swiftly toward a resolution.

April 18, 2005

Anticipation lay like a thick blanket over the day on which the first conclave of the third millennium of Christianity was scheduled to begin. The eligible cardinal-electors of the Roman Catholic church—115 in number (with two absent, unable to travel due to ill health)—rose early for personal prayer, some of them pausing for a light breakfast or coffee. At 10 a.m. they proceeded into the main sanctuary of St. Peter's Basilica, the most recognized church in all the world, for the solemn Eucharistic celebration with the Votive Mass *Pro Eligendo Papa* (For the Election of the Pope). As the apostolic constitution (*Universi Dominici Gregis*, published by John Paul II on February 22, 1996) laid out the procedure: "The celebration should preferably take place at a suitable hour in the morning, so that in the afternoon the prescriptions of the following [sections] of this constitution can be carried out."

The principal celebrant of the liturgy was again the dean of the college of cardinals, Joseph Ratzinger. Having presided at the funeral Mass for the late pontiff, his face was increasingly familiar to the world. The ceremonies were broadcast live via satellite, beginning about 4 a.m. Eastern Daylight Time. From beneath the baldachino, Gian Lorenzo Bernini's soaring bronze masterpiece, Cardinal Ratzinger addressed his fellow princes of the church—and the world—in his homily. The words, spoken in Latin but translated into multiple languages as he delivered them, would receive much attention and comment in the press.

Filled with scriptural references from the readings and demonstrating his mastery of the texts, the cardinal's sermon again reached his primary audience: the men arrayed in semicircular rows, all in blood-red chasubles with white miters. He said:

> How many winds of doctrine we have known in recent
> decades, how many ideological currents, how many ways of
> thinking.... The small boat of thought of many Christians
> has often been tossed about by these waves—thrown from
> one extreme to the other: from Marxism to liberalism, even to
> libertinism; from collectivism to radical individualism; from
> atheism to a vague religious mysticism; from agnosticism to
> syncretism, and so forth. Every day new sects are created and
> what St. Paul says about human trickery comes true, with

cunning which tries to draw those into error [cf, Ephesians 4:14]. Having a clear faith, based on the creed of the church, is often labeled today as a fundamentalism. Whereas relativism, which is letting oneself be tossed and "swept along by every wind of teaching," looks like the only attitude [acceptable] to today's standards. We are moving toward a dictatorship of relativism which does not recognize anything as for certain and which has as its highest goal one's own ego and one's own desires.

However, we have a different goal: the Son of God, true man. He is the measure of true humanism. Being an "adult" means having a faith which does not follow the waves of today's fashions or the latest novelties. A faith which is deeply rooted in friendship with Christ is adult and mature. It is this friendship which opens us up to all that is good and gives us the knowledge to judge true from false and deceit from truth. We must become mature in this adult faith; we must guide the flock of Christ to this faith. And it is this faith—only faith—which creates unity and takes form in love. On this theme, St. Paul offers us some beautiful words—in contrast to the continual ups and downs of those who are like infants, tossed about by the waves: [he says] make truth in love, as the basic formula of Christian existence. In Christ, truth and love coincide. To the extent that we draw near to Christ, in our own life, truth and love merge. Love without truth would be blind; truth without love would be like "a resounding gong or a clashing cymbal" (1 Corinthians 13:1).[1]

THE PROPHECY OF ST. MALACHY
Gloria Olivae

An Irish bishop of the twelfth century, St. Malachy went to Rome on an *ad limina* visit to Pope Innocent II (1130–1143) where he is said to have received a vision of the future popes—until the end of time. The authenticity of the prophecies—often just a few key words in Latin—is questionable, but they are always the subject of analysis and speculation.

The prophecy connected with Pope Benedict XVI's pontificate, the second to last on Malachy's list, is *Gloria Olivae*, "glory of the olives."

The religious order founded by St. Benedict (circa 480–543) has believed that this pope would come from their ranks; one of their sub-orders is the Olivetans. Further, the previous Pope Benedict XV (1914–1922) was called a peacemaker for his efforts to bring an end to World War I (an oblique reference to the olive branch). Benedict XVI has no formal connection with the Benedictine order, but his choice of name honors both the original St. Benedict and the twentieth-century pope.

At the phrase, "dictatorship of relativism," there was a nearly audible gasp along the electronic communications band, among press observers who commented upon the public rituals, analyzed the cardinals' posture, and reported the story, as it was happening.

Ratzinger concluded with words that spoke to the purpose of the day:

> [R]eturning again to the letter to the Ephesians, which says with words from Psalm 68 that Christ, ascending into heaven, "gave gifts to men" (Ephesians 4:8). The victor offers gifts. And these gifts are apostles, prophets, evangelists, pastors,

and teachers. Our ministry is a gift of Christ to humankind,
to build up his body—the new world. We live out our
ministry in this way, as a gift of Christ to humanity! But
at this time, above all, we pray with insistence to the Lord,
so that after the great gift of Pope John Paul II, he again gives
us a pastor according to his own heart, a pastor who guides
us to knowledge in Christ, to his love and to true joy. Amen.

In the afternoon, the body of cardinal electors proceeded into the
Sistine Chapel in pairs, then took their places at the tables lined around
the walls of the chamber where such momentous events had occurred in
past decades and centuries. They placed their red birettas, the familiar,
cornered clerical hats on the tables before them. A choir sang the litany
of the saints, and the Swiss Guard stood at the ready outside the doors.

Cardinal Ratzinger read the oath of secrecy for the last, but not
the first time during the previous ten days. One by one, each cardinal
walked to the open Book of the Gospels and swore to obey the rules,
to keep the secrets—and to serve the church as pope, if elected. For
the first time in history, this segment of the conclave procedure was
broadcast to the world on television.

Archbishop Piero Marini, the veteran master of liturgical ceremonies,
called *"Extra omnes!"* (Everyone out!), the prescribed signal for the doors
to be locked with only the cardinals and some staff members remaining
inside.

That evening, more than two hours after entering the conclave, the
result of the cardinals' vote became visible to the world: first an uncertain wisp (some thought it was white) then a definitive waft of black
smoke. Although a two-thirds consensus on the very first ballot would

be rare, some of the tens of thousands in the square wept. The press retired, girded for a potentially very long conclave.

April 19, 2005

The *Financial Times* of London printed a dramatic cover photograph of Cardinal Ratzinger in St. Peter's before the conclave, and page ten headline reading, "Talents make [Dionigi] Tettamanzi papal frontrunner: Milan archbishop is seen as a leading candidate in his native Italy, but history shows that favorites often lose out." A less spectacular picture of the cardinal accompanied the story. That newspaper, others around the world (especially within Italy itself), and many veteran vaticanists posited the return of an Italian pope—and the popular, jovial archbishop of Milan seemed to be leading the pack in that regard. However, through the preceding week of formal mourning for the deceased pontiff, which ended Saturday, April 16, Cardinal Ratzinger was reported to be steadily gaining in support; he might have forty or fifty votes on the first ballot, some reporters said.

"The conclave is widely expected to require a few days," The *Star-Ledger* (Newark, New Jersey) reported. The Associated Press reported muckraking efforts and gossip-mongering among reporters: "Journalists have been poking around [Cardinal Joseph] Ratzinger's teenage years during World War II, apparently searching for evidence of any pro-Nazi sentiment." The Italian press was rife with reports about the health of various cardinals, including Scola of Venice and Diaz of Bombay.

However, the sentiments of cardinals and close Vatican observers as well as Ratzinger's own strong, prophetic words in the pre-conclave homily led newspapers and wire services to posit Ratzinger as the prohibitive favorite. As the AP wrote: "The 78-year-old Bavarian prelate is the supposed favorite of cardinals leaning toward an elderly figure to lead the church for likely just a few years while churchmen try to absorb the legacy of John Paul's twenty-six years at the helm."

Inside the conclave, as later reported in somewhat oblique terms in the world's press, Ratzinger had received a very substantial number of votes on the first ballot. The balloting on Tuesday morning increased his lead. Several cardinals later commented that the sense of inevitability— not unwelcome—and even divine favor settled upon the rather slight man who possessed the respect and "political" support of more electors each time a vote was taken.

Newsweek quoted Cardinal Cormac Murphy-O'Connor, archbishop of Westminster, England, as saying "there was a gasp all round" when Ratzinger topped the two-thirds mark. *Time* nearly went so far as to call the outcome pre-determined, citing a "stealth campaign" by Roman curial insiders for Ratzinger, against any challenge from "the left." And *U.S. News & World Report*, judiciously suggested a lunchtime "gentlemen's agreement" on Tuesday between Joseph Ratzinger and Carlo Maria Martini, the archbishop emeritus of Milan.

The consensus of the Italian and American journalists, however, is that Cardinals Ratzinger and Martini, both seventy-eight and each representing a somewhat extreme and opposite position along the theological spectrum, achieved about forty votes or one-third apiece on the first ballot, Monday afternoon. Martini, though a sentimental favorite among progressive reformers, was a Parkinson's sufferer and a Jesuit, two big strikes against him (the Jesuits having clashed so publicly with John Paul II). The odds-on Italian favorite, Cardinal Tettamanzi received less than a handful of votes (perhaps as few as two) early on and did not gain any momentum thereafter. The "insiders," members of the Roman Curia, including the vicar of Rome, Cardinal Ruini, stuck with Ratzinger.

The liberals, seeing the futility of a Martini victory, switched to Jorge Bergolio of Argentina, another oft-mentioned *papabile*, but Ratzinger's total vote grew on the second ballot, falling just short of the needed two-thirds—seventy-seven—on the third scrutiny. On ballot four, fewer than twenty cardinals out of 117 did not vote for Ratzinger, giving him an overwhelming total, nearly one hundred votes, in near-record time....

"The liberals were simply out-organized by the Curia," *Time* stated.

The morning newspapers had barely been scanned (on the East coast), and were largely unread in later U.S. time zones, when the news bulletins announced that after less than twenty-four hours (and only four ballots), the work of the college of cardinals was completed. The crowds standing in St. Peter's Square saw the white smoke spew from the chimney above the Sistine Chapel at about 6 p.m. on a drizzly, but hope-filled day. The bells of the basilica chimed shortly thereafter.

At 6:48 p.m. local time, the cardinal deacon proclaimed the "joyful news" that "we have a pope," giving first his Christian name and surname, then his new papal name. The German cardinal—now Holy Father and sovereign of the world's smallest state—stepped forward onto the central balcony in full view of all, attired in the white cassock and zucchetto (skull cap), and wrapped in the scarlet and gold stole. He smiled, clasped his raised hands in a fraternal, "team" gesture, then opened his arms to the city and the world.

Jubilant, and perhaps somewhat shell-shocked at the rapid turn of events that had brought him to this place, Pope Benedict XVI proclaimed the pontifical blessing and briefly addressed the tens of thousands of foreign pilgrims and curious Romans in the piazza. He spoke in Italian:

> Dear brothers and sisters, after the great Pope John Paul II, the cardinals have elected me, a simple and humble laborer in the vineyard of the Lord. The fact that the Lord knows how to work and to act even with inadequate instruments comforts me, and above all I entrust myself to your prayers. Let us move forward in the joy of the risen Lord, confident of his unfailing help. The Lord will help us, and Mary, his most holy mother, will be on our side.

Immediately, the worldwide faithful began to ask, What does he stand for? For American Catholics of a liberal inclination and for many Europeans, Benedict's election portended inflamed doctrinal or "policy" debates. Many viewed him with skepticism, even some U.S. Catholics with outright hostility for his staunch statements and writings on some "hot button" issues. (See Chapter 10 for a discussion of individual issues and where Pope Benedict is likely to stand on each).

On the other hand, the substantial conservative American Catholic community received the announcement of Ratzinger's election with genuine joy and relief. The so-called "Panzer Bishop" and "Pope's Rotweiller" offered reassurance that doctrine—the deposit of faith in preconciliar terminology—remains inviolable. The new pontiff's stinging words on the dangers of relativism and secularism, as well as his history of removing errant Catholic theologians from teaching positions, made him a hero and potential candidate for sainthood.

Response, reaction, instant analysis—liberal and conservative, informed and speculative—was the order of the first day of this just-birthed pontificate. Benedict was immediately hailed (and reviled) as a pontiff for a new, post-John Paul II era.

April 20, 2005

The morning after his election, Pope Benedict XVI concelebrated Mass with the cardinals in the Sistine Chapel. He spoke to them in Latin and immediately began to answer some of the concerns (outlined above) regarding ecumenism, collegiality, and his emerging pastoral style as Holy Father. *The New York Times* called it "a striking shift in tone" from his pre-conclave remarks, his denunciation of a "dictatorship of relativism" and "new sects."

He addressed the "venerable brother cardinals, dear brothers and sisters in Christ, and men and women of good will." Knowing that this first substantive papal statement would signal the direction for his entire pontificate, his opening words bespoke his intentions:

> May grace and peace be multiplied to all of you! In these
> hours, two contrasting sentiments coexist in my spirit. On
> one hand, a sense of inadequacy and of human anxiety before
> the universal Church, because of the responsibility that was
> entrusted to me yesterday as Successor of the Apostle Peter in
> this See of Rome. On the other hand, I feel very intensely in
> myself a profound gratitude to God who—as we sing in the
> liturgy—does not abandon his flock, but leads it through the
> times, under the guidance of those whom he himself has
> chosen as vicars of his Son and has constituted pastors.

Beloved, this profound gratitude for a gift of the divine mercy prevails in my heart despite everything. And I consider it in fact as a special grace obtained for me by my venerated predecessor, John Paul II. I seem to feel his strong hand gripping mine; I seem to see his smiling eyes and to hear his words, addressed at this moment particularly to me: "Do not be afraid!"

To you, Lord Cardinals, with a grateful spirit for the trust shown to me, I ask that you support me with prayer and with constant, active and wise collaboration. I ask also all brothers in the episcopate to be by my side with prayer and counsel, so that I can truly be *Servus servorum Dei.* ["The Servant of the Servants of God," an official papal title since the pontificate of Pope St. Gregory I the Great (590–604).] As Peter and the other apostles constituted, by the will of the Lord, a unique apostolic college, in the same way the Successor of Peter and the bishops, successors of the apostles, must be very closely united among themselves, as the Council confirmed forcefully. [He referred to the Vatican II Constitution on the Church, Lumen Gentium.]

This collegial communion, though in the diversity of roles and functions of the Roman pontiff and of the bishops, is at the service of the Church and of unity in the faith, from which depends in notable measure the efficacy of the evangelizing action in the contemporary world. Therefore, I wish to continue on this path on which my venerated predecessors advanced, concerned only to proclaim to the whole world the living presence of Christ.

GERMAN POPES

After a series of popes from 1032–1046 who were either deposed or expelled from Rome (Benedict IX, Silvester III, Gregory VI), the devout German Emperor Henry III intervened in an attempt to reform the papacy. This resulted in a string of four German popes. Their names consciously recalled the papacy of an earlier, purer church. These Germans were not brought up in the suffocating political atmosphere of Rome.

Clement II
German, from Saxony
Original name: Suidger
Early career: Bishop of Bamberg
Elected pope: December 24, 1046
Died: October 9, 1047 of lead poisoning
Length of pontificate: 9 months, 17 days

Damasus II
German, from Bavaria
Original name: Poppo
Early career: Bishop of Brixen
Elected pope: July 17, 1048
Died: August 9, 1048 at Palestrina, possibly of malaria
Length of pontificate: 23 days

St. Leo IX
German, from Alsace, aristocrat
Original name: Bruno of Egisheim
Early career: Bishop of Toul
Elected pope: February 12, 1049, age 46
Died: April 19, 1054
Length of pontificate: 5 years, 2 months, 7 days

Victor II
German, from Swabia
Original name: Gebhard of Dollnstein-Hirschberg
Early career: Bishop of Eichstatt
Elected pope: April 13, 1055, age about 37
Died: July 28, 1057 of fever
Length of pontificate: 2 years, 3 months, 15 days

Primary sources: P.G. Maxwell-Stuart, *Chronicle of the Popes* (London: Thames & Hudson, 1997); J.N.D. Kelly, *The Oxford Dictionary of Popes* (New York: Oxford University Press, 1986)

Already, in the eyes of some fellow bishops, Benedict had begun to address the problem of collegiality and decentralization of authority in Rome. Then, he struck a welcome chord on the matter of ecumenism, the hope for reconciliation and union among all Christian denominations:

> Theological dialogue is necessary. Also, in-depth knowledge of the historical reasons for choices made in the past is perhaps indispensable. But what is urgent in the main is that "purification of the memory," so many times recalled by John Paul II, which alone can dispose spirits to receive the full truth of Christ. It is before him, Supreme Judge of every living being, that each one of us must place himself, in the awareness of one day having to render an account to him of what one has done or not done for the great good of the full and visible unity of all his disciples.
>
> The present Successor of Peter lets himself be challenged in the first person by this request and is prepared to do all that is in his power to promote the fundamental cause of ecumenism. In the footsteps of his predecessors, he is fully determined to cultivate every initiative that might seem appropriate to promote contacts and understanding with representatives of the diverse churches and ecclesial communities. To them, indeed, he also sends on this occasion the most cordial greeting in Christ, the only Lord of all.[2]

That was grist for days of analysis, especially in light of the response that Cardinal Ratzinger had engendered with the document issued by his Congregation for the Doctrine of the Faith just four years previously,

Dominus Iesu (The Lord Jesus), in which he unequivocally posited the fullness of salvation and revelation within the Catholic Church, above all other Christian communities and all non-Christian faiths.

Pope Benedict set himself a high bar. Would he be able to jump so high so quickly as he seemed to be promising?

Later in the same day, the new pope visited his private apartment, a few blocks from the Vatican, on Piazza della Città Leonina. He greeted passersby and former neighbors and their children. His elderly face, beaming among the people even within a heavy phalanx of security, made the front pages of nearly every major newspaper in the world.

Habemus papam! the faithful exclaimed throughout the globe. We certainly do have a pope...but who is he? Where did he come from?

CHAPTER 6

YOUNG JOSEPH

"I was born on Holy Saturday, April 16, 1927, in Marktl am Inn. The fact that my day of birth was the last day of Holy Week and the eve of Easter has always been noted in our family history. This was connected with the fact that I was baptized immediately on the morning of the day I was born with the water that had just been blessed." In his memoir, *Milestones*, written several years before his election as Pope Benedict XVI, Joseph Ratzinger reflects upon the first fifty years of his life, up to the time of his ordination (also called consecration) as a bishop and installation as archbishop of Munich and Freising on the vigil of Pentecost, May 28, 1977.[1]

His has not been an "action-packed" life (such as that of Karol Wojtyla), yet the milestones and achievements of the man, born the son of a policeman, now, in clear hindsight, seem inevitably to point to his ascension to the Throne of St. Peter at the age of seventy-eight.

A Bavarian Childhood

The elder Joseph Ratzinger was fifty years old when his second son and third child came into the world. Family portraits show a gray man with a cultivated mustache. Maria Ratzinger sits by her husband's side, a small figure, rather plain, with her hair pulled back in the style of an early-century matron. They had three children, Maria, Georg, and Joseph.

The town of his birth lies on the border of Austria in the southeasternmost corner of Germany, but the family often moved, following the father's career as a policeman as he was transferred with regularity until his retirement at the age of sixty. Ratzinger wrote of this period in his life: "It is not at all easy to say what my hometown really is."

Cardinal Ratzinger lived with his family during the 1920s through the 1940s, between the Inn and Salzach Rivers, a mountainous, forested region within Bavaria dotted with small towns clustered near Regensburg. He noted that the local town of Altotting had a long history as a pilgrimage site with a shrine to the Virgin Mary that dated to the time of Charlemagne. His childhood was filled with images of religious houses and churches, holy days, and beautiful Christmases. The family moved to the town of Tittmoning in 1929, then to Traunstein three years later.

In an interview with *The New York Times* shortly after the pope's election, Benedict's elder brother, Father Georg Ratzinger, recalls family events, boyhood dreams, and the early academic career of young Joseph. At age five, the future pontiff encountered Cardinal Michael Faulhaber, the archbishop of Munich (1917–1952) and determined from that moment that he would be a cardinal of the church one day. Though, the *Times* reported, before his meeting with the cardinal, Joseph had "set his heart on becoming a painter." There is no evidence that the boy ever questioned his faith or his true vocation.[2]

Not much is known or has been written (including by Ratzinger himself) of his mother and sister. But his father stands out as a staunch opponent of the Nazi Party on the local level, during elections in the early 1930s. In fact, his conflict with the party played a part in his transfer out of Tittmoning.

Thereafter, Joseph picnicked on the hilltops of the Salzach Valley with his mother, elder sister, and brother. He remembers in particular the Ponlach Chapel, "a lovely Baroque shrine completely surrounded by woods. Near it you can hear the clear waters of the Ponlach rushing down to the valley." Castles and fortresses and the ruins of Roman roads bespoke the glories of the past and gave the youngster a sense of the long history of his region—and his church.

Despite such beautiful scenes, the economic crisis—inflation, depression, poverty—were ever-present in these years. Political unrest fed the political success of Adolf Hitler's anti-communist Nazis. Hitler ran for president of the Reich in 1932, but lost to the elderly military commander of the Great War, Paul von Hindenburg. Joseph's parents rejoiced when Hitler was not elected, but had little confidence in the older leader, as Ratzinger recalls, "since in him they did not see a reliable opponent to the rise of the thuggish brownshirts who dreamed of power. Time and again, in public meetings, Father had to take a position against the violence of the Nazis."

On January 30, 1933, President Hindenburg appointed Hitler chancellor of the German Reich. Soon the Hitler Youth and League of German Girls were introduced as mandatory membership organizations for all young people, and Ratzinger's brother Georg and sister Maria were required to join. He was still a lad of six.

Outside of Traunstein, the Ratzingers lived in the farm town of Aschau am Inn in the second-floor apartment of an old country house above the police headquarters. It was another picturesque German landscape; the house itself had a garden in front and a meadow in back with a pond in which "I almost drowned once while playing," Joseph recalled. A wayside cross—where passersby could stop and pray for a moment—stood in the front garden. Nature and religion were ever combined in the boy's experiences.

War preparations were instituted throughout Germany. In the hills above Traunstein, a lighthouse was built for purposes of sighting enemy aircraft. Later Joseph learned that a secret ammunitions plant was built in a nearby forest, camouflaged and situated so that it could not be spotted from land or air.

Young Joseph's brother became an altar boy and preceded him to school, the humanistic gymnasium, as it was called. There Joseph was exposed to languages, including the Latin that would become such an important tool in his priesthood and theological studies. Then Georg entered the minor seminary (junior high and high school-level) of the archdiocese of Munich, which was in Traunstein. Joseph followed the same course. He entered the boarding school-style minor seminary in 1939, at Easter.

Meanwhile, his sister had received her own high school degree, completed a year's required government service in agriculture, and landed a paying job at a large company, also in Traunstein.

Minor Seminary—and War

At St. Michael School the students followed a strict schedule, waking up at 5 a.m., attending Mass at 6:30, then classes after breakfast until early afternoon, followed by study well into the evening. Joseph was known as an avid student, preternaturally intelligent, who liked books and music (with a special love for Mozart) above athletics and boyish rough-house. Mandatory school games were "torture" for him because he was small, not physically adept, and the youngest of the sixty or so boys at the seminary.

From a very early age, Ratzinger had been enthralled with the church and with all things religious. The liturgical calendar gave shape and meaning and depth to his existence. "The church year gave the time its rhythm, and I experienced that with great gratitude and joy already as a child, indeed, above all as a child," he writes. Advent, Lent, Easter, the Eucharistic liturgy, and the German missal, or prayer book called the *Schott* (named after a Benedictine monk who had translated the text) made deep and lasting impressions upon him.

His studies at the minor seminary opened up even further the colorful world he had discovered in the *Schott* and the liturgies and festivals of boyhood. But the boarding-school atmosphere was difficult for the shy eleven-year-old.

Then came the war. Hitler and Stalin invaded Poland in 1939. Previously, the German dictator's *Anschluss*, or annexation of Austria, had opened the eyes of the people in the region—and around the world—to his boundless territorial ambitions. Now war became a reality for the German people. The school was closed and transformed into a military hospital. Georg and Joseph lived at home and walked to classes in a new location before relocating to a convent that had been closed to nuns by the authorities.

Invasions of France, Scandinavia, the Low Lands, and the Balkans followed, and there seemed to be no stopping Adolf Hitler's *blitzkrieg* throughout 1940 and 1941. In general the mood in Germany was buoyant, patriotic, even for those who were skeptical of National Socialism. Not so in the Ratzinger household: "My father, however, was one who with unfailing clairvoyance saw that a victory of Hitler's would not be a victory for Germany, but rather a victory of the Antichrist that would surely usher in apocalyptic times for all believers, and not only for them."

After Germany's ill-fated attack on Russia in 1941, wounded soldiers arrived by the truckload in the hospital (Joseph's former school) in Traunstein. All available houses and public buildings became hospitals, and Georg and Joseph came back home again. Then, in 1942 Georg was drafted—first into labor service, then into the army of the Third Reich. He was eventually wounded, sent home to convalesce, then shipped out for further service in Italy.

The fourteen-year-old who hoped that he would be spared such a trial, had a "good year" at the gymnasium, studying the Latin and Greek classics. He also began reading German literature and to write a bit himself, including some original translation of religious texts. Touched by the grim reality of war, he nonetheless found escape and solace in his beloved books and studies—for a brief time.

On the day of his election as Benedict XVI, Ratzinger's teenaged affiliation with the Hitler Youth was highlighted in press reports and questions were immediately raised by those who were unfamiliar with the man beyond his image as the "watchdog" or "enforcer" of Catholic doctrine (to use some of the less vitriolic terms). The English newspaper *The Sun* printed this headline: "From Hitler Youth to Papa Ratzi." *The New York Times* handled the potential controversy more gingerly, but with a whiff of potential scandal: "Few See Taint in Service by Pope in Hitler Youth."

What happened? What does it mean for the pope, the papacy, and the Catholic Church that Benedict XVI was, as he acknowledges and explains in his autobiography, a member of the Nazi Party's chief youth organization?

When the organization was established, all high-school age youth were required to join for purposes of indoctrination in Nazi ideology.

First Joseph's brother Georg, being older, was compelled to sign on and attend meetings. Later, in 1941, when he was fourteen, Joseph himself was enrolled as a member by the director of his school. Ratzinger has never denied or obscured this period of his life. There has been no evidence from the time, or subsequently, that he was in thrall to National Socialism or to Hitler or to militarism or super-patriotism.

Ratzinger's family, especially his father, being so staunchly Catholic, opposed the political and social violence espoused by the Nazi Party. Before his retirement, the elder Joseph had been demoted within the police force for his outspoken anti-Nazi sentiments. The village where the family lived, Traunstein, chafed at the anti-clerical, anti-church policies of the Nazis and some two thousand townspeople signed a petition against the removal of crucifixes from schoolrooms, which had been ordered by party officials.

Much later in his life, Joseph Ratzinger would contribute substantially to the church's outreach to Jews and Pope John Paul II's efforts at reconciliation between Catholics and Jews.

From 1943 to 1945, beginning at age sixteen, he saw military service. First, he and other young seminarians (those born in 1926 and 1927) were drafted into the "Flak" or anti-aircraft defense corps. He trained in Munich, lived in barracks, and carried on his studies, albeit a reduced course load, as he recounts in his memoirs. His competitive spirit was kindled, as a youngster from the countryside transferred to the big city. His Latin and Greek skills became a source of pride.

"Our first location was Ludwigsfeld, to the north of Munich, where we had to protect a branch of the Bavarian Motor Works (BMW) that produced motors for airplanes." He endured, formed bonds of friendship with others of his age and circumstance, and attempted to keep up his studies and his practice of the Catholic faith. His group moved to Unterfohring, briefly to Innsbruck, Austria, then to Gilching, north of Lake Ammer.

A picture of Joseph during his wartime service, in cap, tie, and military jacket, shows a smooth-faced youth with the deep-set eyes and dark brow that are familiar to this day in photographs of the mature, now elderly prelate. He looks neither unhappy nor particularly pleased, rather serenely determined to survive—perhaps so that he could read more Goethe, hear more Mozart, and study more Scripture. More trials lay ahead.

Early in 1944 he indeed survived a direct attack on his battery. Through the summer he traveled back and forth to Munich for studies, despite the bombing raids on the city. Then, on September 10, 1944, he was released from the Flak. He returned to his family's home briefly, for he found a draft notice for the *Reichsarbeitdienst*, the national labor force. He was assigned to a camp that was located at the place where the borders of Austria, Hungary, and Czechoslovakia (all under German occupation) met.

These times of increasing gloom at the approach of certain defeat left him, he writes, "with oppressive memories."

Work and indoctrination filled the endless days of the young "volunteers." SS officers and party fanatics supervised the workers, preaching a cult of work as redemptive. It was far better than the death camps that thrived under the criminal regime's occupation of Europe, but the teenagers inside the camp did not know that. Their spades were more than tools, they were objects of veneration that must be spotless when not in use; there were prescribed drills and rituals for how to dig, how to hold and lay down the spade.

An End to War, A New Beginning

Ratzinger recalls that his outward intention to become a priest led to his ostracism from the inner circle that ran like a street gang. He was mocked and insulted, yet freed from the intense pressure of being part of the ruling group. However, a few comrades kept him from being completely alone, and prayer helped him retain his sanity.

Another swift turn of events: Soviet troops overran Hungary. The Third Reich had begun to crumble. He and his cohorts were called back to Munich for another assignment. Joseph returned to Traunstein, assigned to the infantry barracks there; he took a brief leave at home before reporting for duty. He and other barracks-mates celebrated Christmas 1944. Some of his comrades were in their forties, others were little older than schoolboys, like himself. Of the older soldiers, he writes: "My heart was deeply moved by their homesickness for wives and children."

He was never called from Traunstein to the front. In May 1945, young Joseph deserted his post and returned to his parents' home nearby. His parents and sister were safe, but there had been no word of his brother Georg since April. Within weeks the Americans occupied the town, and Joseph Ratzinger was captured as a prisoner of war.

Before he was marched away from his mother and father, he slipped a notebook and pencil into his pocket. He marched for three days to the military airport of Bad Aibling, then was shipped to Ulm along with about fifty thousand other prisoners. They slept outdoors and survived on "one ladleful of soup and a little bread per day." After a few days of good weather, the rains soaked all who were unfortunate enough to have no shelter. The sight of the majestic cathedral of Ulm on the near horizon gave him some hope amid the chaos and discomfort of POW life.

At this time, he discovered that there were other seminarians such as himself, and Catholic priests who were able to offer Mass for the prisoners. There were also university professors among the throng, who quickly arranged academic conferences to keep the prisoners occupied, alert, and learning. The weeks passed in this way, and Joseph filled his notebook with thoughts and experiences. He made friends and held onto his faith.

Starting in June, some of the prisoners were released. On June 19, Joseph Ratzinger, a veteran of two years military service, now age eighteen, was set free. "I held in my hand," he records, "the certificate of release that made the end of the war a reality for me, too." He was transported to Munich, then walked and hitchhiked aboard a milk truck with a companion. On the evening of the Feast of the Sacred Heart of Jesus he arrived at his parents' home.

Still, there was no news, official or otherwise, about his brother Georg. The family's happiness and relief for Joseph remained muted until, a month later, the elder brother returned, sporting a "brown tan from the Italian sun."

Both brothers were destined for the priesthood. Over the next several months they enjoyed the relative security of the postwar situation and became reacquainted with neighbors and friends—and each other. They helped restore the minor seminary buildings where they had been students, and which had been used as a hospital for wounded German soldiers. This time they were an enthusiastic labor brigade, working for a cause in which they believed.

That autumn the brothers moved to Freising to enter the major seminary. That campus, too, served as a military hospital, so they were set up in temporary living and classroom accommodations. According to Ratzinger's autobiography, 120 seminarians enrolled in this first group since war's end. They were a diverse lot, ranging in age from teens to early forties. Some had served in the military for the entire duration of the conflict, others, like young Joseph, had seen limited service. All were deeply affected, whether by physical privation or psychological scars, by loss of comrades-in-arms or family members. They had known danger, injury, starvation, and confinement; many had been separated for years from regular church attendance or religious observance, except what an individual might muster on the battlefield or on the home front.

His Great Awakening

Joseph Ratzinger's childhood dream, his commitment to the vocation of the priesthood was to be fulfilled. With enthusiasm he entered into the seminary community. The Nazi purges of seminaries and university, as well as Allied bombing, had damaged libraries and halted regular book publication throughout Germany. But the Freising seminary still possessed a decent reference collection. Books were shared. Joseph and his fellows read widely in philosophy and theology.

Alfred Lapple, later to become a widely respected religious writer and thinker, became prefect of Joseph's hall. Lapple directed the student's reading program: metaphysics, science, the philosophical foundations of moral theology; authors such as Heidegger, Husserl, Newman, Nietzsche, and Bergson. Ratzinger discovered Martin Buber and delved into St. Augustine. Of the thirteenth-century giant who loomed over all of Catholic theology, he wrote in his memoirs: "By contrast [with Augustine], I had difficulties in penetrating the thought of Thomas Aquinas, whose crystal-clear logic seemed to me to be too closed in on itself, too impersonal and ready-made."

A CHRONOLOGY OF BENEDICT XVI'S LIFE

1927: April 16, Joseph Ratzinger is born in Marktl am Inn, Germany, the son of Joseph, a policeman, and Maria, and younger brother of Maria and Georg.

1929: His family moves to the town of Tittmoning on border of Austria.

1932: His family moves to Auschau am Inn, after his father has conflicts with local Nazi Party supporters in Tittmoning.

1937: His father retires from active service as a policeman, and he continues schooling; family moves to Hufschlag, outside of Traunstein.

1939: He enters the minor seminary in Traunstein, St. Michael School, following footsteps of his brother.

1941: Enrolled against his will in Hitler Youth while at seminary, he is dismissed shortly afterward because of his intention to study for the priesthood.

1943: Drafted as a helper for the Flak, an anti-aircraft unit, he serves in a battery defending a BMW plant.

1944: September 10, he is dismissed from his unit, but returns home to find a draft notice for forced labor.
September 20, he leaves home to dig anti-tank trenches.
November 20, he is released from the labor force and returns home, only to receive an army draft notice three weeks later.

1945: April–May, he deserts from the army and returns home. Joseph is captured by Americans as the war ends.
June 19, he is released from a U.S. POW camp and hitchhikes home on a milk truck.
November, he begins formation for the priesthood in Friesing.

1947: He enters theological institute, Georgianum, affiliated with University of Munich.

1951: June 29 (Feast of Saints Peter and Paul), he is ordained a priest in Munich, Germany, along with his elder brother Georg.

1953: He receives a doctorate in theology from the University of Munich based on prize-winning essay on St. Augustine.

1959: April 15, he begins teaching theology in Bonn as dogmatic theology chair, the first of several appointments in German universities.
August 23, his father, Joseph, dies.

1962–1965: The priest-theologian participates in all four sessions of Vatican II Council in Rome, as *peritus* (adviser) to Cardinal Joeph Frings of Cologne.

1963: He takes a position at University of Munster.
December 16, his mother, Maria, dies.

1966: Takes chair in dogmatic theology at University of Tübingen.

1968: Student uprisings occur across Europe, including Tübingen. He sees Marxism become the dominant political ideology in universities.

1969: He leaves the University of Tübingen, concerned about student unrest which had interrupted his lectures with sit-ins and takes a teaching job in Regensburg in native Bavaria, near his brother.

1970: He builds a home near Regensburg as retreat and family gathering place.

1972: With leading theologians, Hans Urs von Balthasar and Henri de Lubac, he founds theological journal *Communio*.

1977: March 14, he is named archbishop of Munich and Freising and exactly two months later, is ordained a bishop and installed as metropolitan ordinary.
June 27, he receives red hat of a cardinal and is appointed cardinal-priest of S. Maria Consolatrice al Tiburtino.

1980: He declines Pope John Paul II's invitation to head Congregation for Catholic Education in Roman Curia.

1981: November 25, he is appointed president of International Theological Commission, prefect of Doctrine of the Faith, and president of Pontifical Biblical Commission, Roman Curia.

1982: February 15, he resigns as archbishop of Munich and Freising.

1993: April 5, he is appointed cardinal-bishop of Velletri-Segni.

2002: November 30, is appointed cardinal-bishop of Ostia and becomes dean of the college of cardinals.

2005: April 2, at the death of Pope John Paul II, he resigns as prefect of Doctrine of the Faith, president of International Theological Commission, and president of Pontifical Biblical Commission, Roman Curia.
April 19, he is elected bishop of Rome by his fellow cardinals on fourth ballot of conclave and takes the name Benedict XVI.
April 24, he is formally installed as pope, accepts the Ring of the Fisherman and the pallium of his office.

It was not for lack of trying. And the seminarian, like his fellow students and eventual candidates for ordination, was hungry for knowledge, energized by hope for the future, grateful to be alive.

The rector of the seminary, Michael Hock, had been imprisoned in the Dachau concentration camp for five years and impressed the students with his humility and ease. The remote figure of Cardinal Faulhaber, the archbishop of Munich-Freising, who had so impressed the five-year-old Joseph Ratzinger, was later termed by critics at best an ambiguous figure during World War II, at worst an accommodator of the Nazis. But Joseph still revered the old prelate, who would remain in the archiepiscopal cathedra for several more years, and whom the future cardinal and pope credited with resisting Nazi encroachments in the theological realm.

Because the war and the Nazi regime had decimated other universities and seminaries, the newly reopened Georgianum in Munich drew distinguished faculty from institutions that no longer existed: from Breslau, Munster, and Braunsberg. The seminary had relocated to an old castle once occupied by the insane King Otto of Germany (who lived into the twentieth century), in suburban Furstenried. Students slept in bunk beds, and faculty members lived in the same building. Lectures were held in the greenhouse, a picturesque setting, but frigid in winter and steaming in summer. The young scholar drank in the teaching and relished the varieties of styles and expertise the professors brought to bear in his studies. He strolled in the overgrown gardens of the castle thinking great thoughts and saying his prayers.

He characterized Friedrich Wilhelm Maier, professor of New Testament, as the preeminent lecturer and scholar among the faculty. As a younger man in the first decade of the twentieth century, he had proposed the famous theory of the "Q" (from *Quelle*) source of the Gospels, which combined the first-written, Mark, with a non-extant compilation of Jesus' sayings. Revolutionary at the time and considered far too "liberal" a theory of exegesis, the teachings got Maier removed from the academy. He served as a military chaplain in World War I, then a prison chaplain. He had been recalled to teaching in 1924, though embittered by his treatment by the Magisterium in Rome (and Archbishop Faulhaber). Maier served as a bridge between the old theology—and old teaching methods—and the new approaches to Scripture as represented by Bultmann and Barth.

The Old Testament professor, Friedrich Stummer, stood in contrast to Maier with his reserved style and painstaking scholarship; no great breakthroughs, instead a thorough exegetical exercise that opened up the Jewish Scripture for the young German students. To Joseph Ratzinger and his fellow seminarians, in a literal "hothouse" of theological scholarship, "the Bible spoke to us with new immediacy and freshness."

There were currents of change, even radicalism in this environment. The "war" between liberalism and conservatism was happening, even as young Joseph was receiving the technical foundation of his own theological career. He recalls that this era, which is often referred to as a kind of dark ages by Catholics in Europe and North America, was instead—in his own experience—a fertile and frantic time of new questions and deep spirituality. The church came alive to him in new ways, such as in the liturgy, which became a lifelong interest and will be one of the theological loci of his pontificate. The pre-Vatican II Catholic theological world, free of war and oppression in Europe, blossomed as so many wildflowers on the academic landscape.

Joseph genuinely enjoyed the olio of city life and seminary studies in a quaint old castle, the contrasts between the secular world and the more insular environment in which the "historical method" vied with pronunciamentos from the Vatican. In 1950 the dogma of the assumption of the Blessed Virgin Mary was defined by Pope Pius XII (that is, the teaching that the mother of Christ was assumed wholly and bodily into heaven). Young Ratzinger participated in and observed the debates that occurred before the doctrine was infallibly proclaimed—the first time since 1854, and the first time since the First Vatican Council (which had defined papal infallibility) that a pope had spoken *ex cathedra* on such a point of the faith. And it is the last time to date that such a doctrine has been put forth.

By 1949 a habitable building had finally been constructed for the Georgianum, and the seminary was relocated to Munich proper. The young scholars, most of them now less than two years from their priestly ordination, left Furstenried behind but kept the memories of that unique time of "great awakening" always intact in their minds.

CHAPTER 7

PRIEST AND SCHOLAR

"The very situation of the priest is singular, alien to modern society. A function, a role that is not based on the consent of the majority but on the representation of another who lets a man share his authority appears as something incomprehensible." Cardinal Joseph Ratzinger spoke these words about the Catholic priesthood to journalist Vittorio Messori in an interview that was published as *The Ratzinger Report* in 1985, twenty years before his election as pope—and twenty years after the Second Vatican Council (1962–1965).[1]

At that time he spoke sharply against priests becoming mere social arbiters or political infighters; rather, they should "abandon themselves" to the higher, divine power they have been chosen to represent in the church on earth. While ever mindful of the sacred and mysterious nature of this peculiar vocation, Ratzinger conducted himself throughout his priesthood as an open, down-to-earth, hard-working, scholarly, and pastoral man.

Holy Orders

For the twenty-four-year-old Joseph, the sacrament of Holy Orders—ordination to the priesthood—had been a lifelong goal and calling. His final year in seminary was one of intense study, writing, and preparation for the day that would transform his life. He passed his final examinations in the summer of 1950, embarked upon the research and writing of a prize essay (the winner would be accepted as a doctoral dissertation), was ordained as a deacon in October, then returned to Freising with the other ordinands to absorb some of the "practical aspects of the priestly ministry": catechesis (teaching the faith), homiletics (preaching sermons), liturgy, and parish administration. While covering important subjects, this course of study provided a welcome break from hardcore academics.

Meanwhile, he was still working on the prize theme that he hoped would win *summa cum laude* honors and open the door to his doctorate. He credited his housemates and especially his brother Georg with helping clear his path of mundane chores, so that he might concentrate on writing. His elder sister, Maria, who was employed as a legal secretary, typed and retyped clean copies of the manuscript.

Then, on June 29, 1951, the Feast of Saints Peter and Paul, Cardinal Faulhaber ordained forty men to the priesthood in the elaborate, moving rite that has been used in the church for centuries. In *Milestones*, Ratzinger writes, "At the moment when the elderly archbishop laid his hands on me, a little bird—perhaps a lark—flew up from the high altar in the cathedral and trilled a little joyful song. And I could not but see in this a reassurance from on high."

The brothers, Georg and Joseph, celebrated their first Mass at their own parish church of St. Oswald in Traunstein. On the occasion and in the immediate days afterward, an overwhelming joy filled Joseph Ratzinger's spirit. He knew he had been transformed, somehow, that he had been marked by his God for a special purpose. Yet he also understood that it was not about *him*, per se. The priest is the vehicle through which Christ can touch other men and women; the priest is Christ's vicar (or stand-in). Virtually all in the village came to the brother priests with friendly meals, requests for blessings, signs of support and affection. And the brothers responded with enthusiasm. Ratzinger was learning, in his own hometown, how to be a priest.

Father Joseph was assigned to be assistant pastor (parochial vicar) of the Church of the Precious Blood in Munich on August 1, 1951. The parish straddled the city line, with much of its territory in a residential suburb. There, factory workers, domestic servants, and shopkeepers, as well as "intellectuals, artists, and high government officials" lived and worshiped together in their parish church. He was quite fortunate to have a supportive boss, his pastor, Father Blunschein—by all accounts a good and humble priest.

Ratzinger encountered what nearly all new priests do: a crushing workload of unfamiliar tasks and responsibilities. Every day but Sunday—including four hours on Saturday—he heard countless confessions. On Sunday he celebrated two masses and gave at least two different homilies (not an easy task for one as obsessed with words as this young cleric). During the week he taught schoolchildren for sixteen hours, along with the usual funeral Masses, burials, baptisms, weddings, youth group meetings, and so forth. It was a never-ending grind, but the freshly ordained priest followed the example of his pastor; he neither flagged in his duties, nor complained.

He especially enjoyed and valued the religious instruction of children. His work as a youth minister quickly made him feel like a part of the parish community. Fresh in his memory were the dark days of his own youth under the shadow of Nazism and during a time of ugly tensions between church and state. The postwar period of "changing circumstances" called for "new forms" and methods for catechesis and evangelization. There was no greater proponent of new ways and new ideas than Father Joseph.

In *Principles of Catholic Theology,* Cardinal Ratzinger wrote of Holy Orders, the Catholic priesthood, as "the sacramental expression of the principle of Tradition," differentiating the priestly ministry from Protestant and other non-Catholic ministries. He holds to the traditional Catholic position that flowed from the councils of Florence, Trent, and Vatican II. Simply put, the bishops are successors to the apostles, those personally chosen by Jesus of Nazareth to follow him and to form the assembly of believers (under the guidance and inspiration of the Holy Spirit) after him. The priest (or presbyter) is the bishop's arm at the local (diocesan and parish) level. The bishop holds the fullness of Holy Orders, the priest is subordinate to his bishop. The priest is a "mediator" and "minister" of Jesus Christ. One could say that the priest is an essential cog in the machinery of the church, by divine intention.

Ratzinger's parish experience was brief. On October 1, 1952, he returned to the seminary in Freising—a bittersweet turn of events for Ratzinger at age twenty-five: "On the one hand this...would enable me to return to my theological work, which I loved so much. On the other hand...I even began to think I would have done better to remain in parish work."[2] The intimate contact with others in pastoral ministry had moved him deeply and filled him with spiritual purpose. He knew the value and rewards of service to others, of being needed, of administering the sacraments—all of which gave him "a joy in the priesthood" that he did not expect to find in the new academic assignment. Yet he was, and always would be, obedient to the call of his vocation as teacher. ...ests called to ministries other than the parish often experience inner conflicts; Ratzinger was no different. His brother has remained a parish priest for his entire adult life in Bavaria where he grew up. However, Joseph would never be simply a parish priest ever again.

Academic Storm Clouds

He embarked upon a new phase in his priesthood: lectures at the seminary, liturgical services, and sitting for more hours in the confessional—but (significantly) in the cathedral church. He did retain involvement with the cathedral's youth group, which he found gratifying, even though it was difficult to squeeze it into his schedule. Having won the prize for his much-labored-over essay, he now faced eight hours of oral examinations plus a written examination to receive his doctorate. In addition he would be required to participate in an open debate ranging across all theological disciplines. The rigorous preparations and exams culminated in his reception of the cap of doctor of theology in July 1953, in the presence of his mother and father, brother and sister.

The habilitation is a post-doctoral degree, which qualifies one to hold a chair at a German university. To obtain such an advanced degree is yet another arduous process, which would require of Father Joseph Ratzinger many months of study and preparation. However, the chair for dogmatic and fundamental theology at the College for Philosophy and Theology in Freising became vacant. An older priest, who had held the chair while trying simultaneously to achieve his own habilitation (a nearly impossible task), had been transferred to yet another chair, in East Germany. The faculty at Freising, who knew young Ratzinger's work and knew him personally, wanted him to fill the position. Ratzinger attempted to delay the appointment for a year—and succeeded. Father Viktor Schurr, whom Joseph had not known until that time, accepted the chair for a one-year appointment (winning Ratzinger's friendship), thus making it possible for the newly minted doctor of theology to spend the necessary time ("leisure," as he wryly called it) to lay the foundation for his next step.

Father Ratzinger, who had focused on patristic theology (that is, the study of early-century church fathers, St. Augustine in particular), now turned to the period of the Middle Ages and chose to work on St. Bonaventure, a formidable theologian and doctor of the church, and the theme of divine revelation. In his memoirs, Ratzinger writes, "I was to try to discover whether in Bonaventure there was anything corresponding to the concept of salvation history, and whether this motif— if it should exist—had any relationship with the idea of revelation." It was a tough topic for anyone to tackle.

The scholar was not unfamiliar with his subject, but needed to delve ever deeper into the writings of the thirteenth-century scholasticist. Bonaventure had been a contemporary of St. Thomas Aquinas, who had notoriously entangled the younger Ratzinger in his early seminary studies. By the summer of 1954, Ratzinger felt he had written enough of the basic outline to lay the foundation for the book-length thesis that was required for the post-doctoral degree. He accepted the chair for dogma at Freising, then (due to the death of one of the elderly professors) found an available, affordable residence. He began lecturing in the winter semester (starting in October). "All of this was happening too fast for me, especially since I still had to do the main part of the work for my habilitation," he recounts in *Milestones*.

For the next year, he faced an unrelenting schedule of lecturing and writing. He found the subject matter of his teaching and the openness and enthusiasm of his students to be refreshing and inspiring. In photographs of the period, Joseph appears as intense, scholarly, priestly— dressed in black with a sliver of white showing on his Roman-style collar. His shock of hair, which would eventually turn gray, then white, over the course of his life, is longish, combed back from his forehead, a bit unruly. The ageless dark eyes remain his intense signature.

Throughout his priesthood, later during his episcopate as archbishop, then as a cardinal and prefect of one of the Vatican's largest congregations (as well as numerous other special assignments for the pope), Ratzinger developed the reputation of being a hard worker and extremely quick study; a good listener, and a fluent talker with well-thought-out words and impeccable theological content. There was no personal flamboyance or "edge" to the man, younger or older.

Throughout the spring and summer of 1955 he redoubled his efforts at writing the book-length thesis for the advanced degree. He employed a typist who turned out to be slow and sloppy, losing handwritten pages and causing the priest-professor to duplicate some of his work. But by the fall he had a completed typescript that he submitted with a sigh of relief. He waited.

Meanwhile, he and his siblings were also concerned about their now-elderly parents. His father was seventy-eight and his mother seventy-one in 1955. They had lived in the same country home outside of Traunstein for nearly a quarter century. The winters were taking their toll, since church and shops were in town and required the couple to travel a two-kilometer distance, "and this was no easy thing, especially in the Traunstein winters, with huge amounts of snow and often frozen streets."

The solution was to move the parents to Freising, where all three children were or planned to be. So in November, Joseph and Maria came to live with their up-and-coming younger son, Joseph. The future cardinal paints a lovely picture of Mother in apron and Father unpacking and smoothing the transition. Georg and Maria joined the household at Christmastime, uniting the family once more.

A storm cloud was about to burst over Father Joseph. One of the two readers of his habilitation manuscript rejected it, after the other had accepted, even praised it and quoted it in his lectures. In the spring of 1955, the priest-scholar was rocked by the potentially disastrous end to his nascent academic career. At Easter he was working productively with fellow theologians on a new conference in Konigstein. There he befriended Karl Rahner, one of the few theological giants of the second half of the twentieth century who would compare with Benedict XVI and John Paul II in terms of impact on Catholic thought. It was then that Ratzinger received the news from his second reader. His thesis was dead in the water. Why? he wondered.

As he explains in his autobiography, first, he had not paid proper obeisance to the elder scholar, who had been a leading light on the pre-World War II scene. In his own researches, Ratzinger had turned some of those earlier theories of revelation on their heads. "With a forthrightness not advisable in a beginner, I criticized the superseded positions, and this was apparently too much" for the established professor. The latter faulted the younger man's analysis, his scholarly methods, and even his presentation. The manuscript also contained errors that Ratzinger had not properly corrected.

Ratzinger was labeled "dangerous" and a "modernist" by some elders in the German academic community. At a faculty meeting to discuss the thesis, Father Joseph gained a reprieve—the manuscript was returned for revision, not rejected outright. His opponents predicted it would take years to correct and resubmit the thesis. But when he finally was able to review the critical notations, Father Ratzinger found them easy to address. He decided to expand the one section of the book that had not been savaged by his critic's pen. In a two-week period, he chopped and rewrote and re-presented the work. On February 11, 1957, he learned that his habilitation thesis was accepted, that now only one more step remained: a public lecture and defense of his work. It was the centuries-old method of "disputation" that had been practiced in European theological circles since before Aquinas.

During the event, a dispute erupted between the two opposing readers of Ratzinger's manuscript. He left the stage. When it was over the dean came out into the hallway to inform him that he had passed the final phase and had earned his habilitation.

Career in Ascendancy

Ratzinger himself quickly soared to star status. Various universities began to vie for his services, not unlike a free-agent in professional sports. He represented the best, the cutting edge of post-war theology and was considered one of the very brightest young progressives in the field.

In summer 1958 his fondest ambition was realized: he was invited to take the chair in fundamental theology in Bonn (the cold war capital of West Germany). He faced a difficult decision, however: if he moved on, his elderly parents would also have to move from their comfortable new situation in Joseph's home. His brother Georg—and perhaps providence—intervened. Georg had finished his graduate studies in music and was assigned to the parish back in Traunstein, St. Oswald. He was able to secure a residence in the center of town, where their mother and father could easily and conveniently live.

Father Ratzinger was relieved and somewhat guilt-ridden over the whole thing. He had become very attached to Freising, to the university, the students, the house, the circle of friends he had developed—and it was the site of his greatest challenge and greatest triumph to date. The University of Bonn represented the "big time," and he was confident enough and ambitious enough, to realize that if his academic reputation and career were to reach ever-higher levels, it was a move he must make.

Immediately, before his thirty-second birthday, he began lecturing in halls filled beyond capacity. He loved the town, the university, the community of scholars and students. From his home state of Bavaria, a place of sturdy farmers and pastoral beauty, he had come to a bustling port on the Rhine River, a cosmopolitan melting pot with several theological colleges (operated by religious orders such as the Dominicans, Redemptorists, and Missionaries of the Divine Word). Among the Franciscan community he met a Bonaventure specialist with whom he broke bread and became fast friends.

Some of the very greatest old names in twentieth-century theology were still teaching, writing, and practicing their scholarly arts: Hubert Jedin, historian of the church councils; Johan Auer, dogma specialist; Theodor Klauser, founding editor of an influential journal. Across disciplines, too, he found kindred spirits, such as the Lutheran scholar Paul Hacker. Ratzinger's own enthusiasm and work ethic impressed his elders and won him "fans" among the student population. He called his first semester in Bonn "one ongoing honeymoon."

In the summer, however, his father suffered a minor stroke—"while carrying my sister's heavy typewriter to the repair shop on a very hot day." He recovered, and the family spent a happy Christmas together in Traunstein. The following August, after a series of strokes, Joseph's father died at the age of eighty-one.

CHAPTER 8

FROM COUNCIL
TO EPISCOPACY

If the passing of John Paul II and the election of Benedict XVI comprised a great theological *moment*, that is, an opportunity for Catholics to gain a better understanding of their faith—then the Second Ecumenical Council of the Vatican, held from 1962 to 1965, was the great theological *event* that will continue to define the church and set its course for the next pontificate and beyond.

Benedict may be the last pope who was a participant in the council. Certainly his contribution to it as well as the council's documents and decrees, loom as large on the horizon of faith as ever and have not receded into the past as some observers and critics may have hoped.

The Tipping Point

In his memoirs[1], Joseph Ratzinger alludes to a strained relationship with one of the participants, Cardinal Joseph Wendl, archbishop of Munich and Freising (1952–1960). He had, however, a close relationship with Cardinal Joseph Frings, archbishop of Cologne (1942–1969), based on Ratzinger's groundbreaking work and an ongoing dialogue between the two men "that became the starting point of a collaboration that lasted for years." Cardinal Frings served on the central preparatory commission for the council and received the draft *schemata* (texts) that would serve as basis for discussion among the council fathers (the Catholic bishops from around the world).

By this time, in the very early 1960s, Father Joseph Ratzinger's network of friends and colleagues in the theological community were well placed throughout the German Catholic church. Some of those friends eventually became bishops themselves, and served during this time as secretaries and advisers to the senior prelates such as Wendl and Frings. Ratzinger continued as a faculty member at Bonn throughout 1963, by which time the council was well under way.

Pope John XXIII, having been elected in 1958 as a presumed "transitional" figure (he was 77 years old and not particularly healthy), shocked the college of cardinals—and the Catholic world—by calling for a general council of the church in short order. It would be the first such meeting of the world's Catholic episcopacy—some 2,500 bishops—since the First Council of the Vatican, which had met in 1869 and 1870, ending prematurely with the Italian army's takeover of the city of Rome during the Franco-Prussian war. Pius IX (1846–1878, the longest-serving pontiff on historical record) then became a self-styled "prisoner of the Vatican," as did his successors until the 1929 concordat with Mussolini's Italian government, which restored sovereign power to the pope and granted territorial integrity to the 109-acre Vatican City State.

The ecclesiological issues of Vatican I, which had been convoked to update and codify the understanding of the church in more modern terms, remained mostly undiscussed and unresolved. That council is most famous—or infamous—for its definition of papal infallibility when the pope teaches *ex cathedra* (from the chair) on matters of faith and morals. To this day, some Catholics and many non-Catholics chafe at this concept—just as many did at the time of that council!

Nonetheless, the decisions and documents of an ecumenical council are considered binding upon the faithful, ever since the first council, in Nicea in 325, at which the creed that Catholics proclaim at Sunday Mass was agreed upon. Before the east-west schism of 1054, when the Orthodox and Latin branches of the church split, the general councils were truly "ecumenical" (universal), even dominated by the churches of the east. Since then, the councils have been papal in nature, convoked by the bishop of Rome and attended by bishops of the Latin or western churches who remain in communion with the Holy Father.

There was no shortage of theological complications and ideological byways. But the entire Christian world anticipated this second council to be held in the Vatican. And men like Joseph Ratzinger, who would be *periti* (theological experts and advisers to their bishops) certainly looked forward to the opportunity to participate in the epochal event. They were also concerned, to a greater or lesser degree, that the council fathers should not go off in any radical direction, given the conservative-progressive fault lines that had become more glaringly apparent with the passage of time.

Ratzinger identified early on the tensions between scholars like himself and "shepherds" concerned with the pastoral care of the faithful. He noted that the "renewal" of theology in prior decades was not always taken into account in the pre-council period, especially concerning biblical studies and patristics (that is, study of early-century church fathers as opposed to Thomas Aquinas neo-scholasticism, which dominated the seminaries and universities). He thought, however, that the documents prepared for the council displayed a solid theological foundation.

Cardinal Frings of Cologne took his secretary, Father Hubert Luthe, a friend of Joseph's from Furstenried, and Father Joseph Ratzinger, as his theological adviser, to Rome in October 1962. Ratzinger's status as a *peritus* was made official before the end of the first session of the council. During this period he lived in the German priests' residence near the Piazzo Navona and rubbed shoulders with, according to his memoirs, "great men like Henri de Lubac, Jean Danielou, and Gerard Philips, to name only a few." Thus, he was to have a front-row seat at the council and a chance to engage in the dialogue of history, which so intrigued and inspired him. The Joseph Ratzinger of the council period developed an interest in a legitimate plurality of theologies and took greater account of historical development in theology.

With pomp and great expectations, the Second Ecumenical Council of the Vatican opened on October 11, 1962. Pope John XXIII presided briefly at the inaugural session, then retreated to allow the council fathers to conduct business without his looking over their shoulders.

Ratzinger's contributions were numerous and have yet to be fully catalogued and interpreted. His unfolding pontificate will tell the world at large much about his personal experience of the council and his thinking, which now only professional theologians can discuss with confidence.

Looking back with journalist Vittorio Messori in *The Ratzinger Report*, Cardinal Ratzinger discussed whether or not he had changed his views since the Vatican Council, as he is often accused of turning from "progressive" to "archconservative." His former friend, the prominent liberal German theologian Hans Kung, said of Ratzinger's seeming turn to the right, "He sold his soul for power."

In response, Ratzinger, who won the esteem of the council fathers and his fellow experts, later said of the charge:

It is not I who have changed, but others. At our very first meetings I pointed out two prerequisites to my colleagues. The first one: our group must not lapse into any kind of sectarianism or arrogance, as if we were the new, the true church, an alternative magisterium with a monopoly on the truth of Christianity. The second one: discussion has to be conducted without any individualistic flights forward, in confrontation with the reality of Vatican II with the true letter and the true spirit of the council, not with an imaginary Vatican III. ...I have always tried to remain true to Vatican II, to this *today* of the church, without any longing for a *yesterday* irretrievably gone with the wind and without any impatient thrust toward a *tomorrow* that is not ours.[2]

Revelation and Faith

Pope John had given the world's bishops only an outline, a general direction, and left it up to the council fathers themselves to find their way, with "almost unlimited freedom to give things concrete shape." Ratzinger saw that the pope remained committed to the unchanging deposit of faith, which must be proclaimed to a contemporary era in a new way, no longer defensively, but with arms open to those who sought to know Jesus Christ in and through the Catholic Church.

He was surprised that the *schema* on liturgy received as much attention and fostered as much debate as it did. This was one of the unexpected effects of the council: to introduce substantial changes in the ways that the Mass was celebrated in countries and cultures throughout the world. It was the end of the Latin-language Mass as the only way, which has ever since caused friction and misunderstanding among Catholics—though the intention was quite the opposite.

The document on the subject of revelation, *Dei Verbum* (The Voice of God), the Dogmatic Constitution on Divine Revelation, was one of the major doctrinal statements of Vatican II. Ratzinger became known ever after as one of the important interpreters of and commentators on this signal product of the council. "Revelation," he writes in *Milestones*, "which is to say, God's approach to man, is always greater than what can be contained in human words, greater even than the words of Scripture.... Revelation is something alive, something grater and *more*....Revelation is not a meteor fallen to earth that now lies around somewhere as a rock mass from which rock samples can be taken and submitted to laboratory analysis." For Ratzinger, and for the Catholic Church, God's revelation continues in the life of the church, through the Holy Spirit, in the work of the Magisterium (once headed by Cardinal Ratzinger). This is the classic argument against the Lutheran appeal to *sola Scriptora* (Scripture alone), and for Ratzinger and the council fathers, it is a matter of core doctrine, a foundational teaching upon the truth and reality upon which the church is built.

At one point Cardinal Frings asked Father Ratzinger to write up a schema to express his view on revelation. He reached out to his friend, Karl Rahner, to help draft something worthy of the bishops' and cardinals' reading in a relatively quick period of time. "As we worked together," Ratzinger recalls, "it became obvious to me that, despite our agreement in many desires and conclusions, Rahner and I lived on two different theological planes." Rahner was the quintessential speculative theologian. The schema became Rahner's alone and was rejected by the council as the official text.

In the summer of 1963 Ratzinger left Bonn to take a lecturer's position in Munster. Later that year, on December 16, his mother, Maria, passed away of cancer. His brother Georg moved to the cathedral city of Regensberg to become director of the choir there. Joseph still faced two more years' work at the council, which meant dividing his time between Munster and Rome.

On the effect of Benedict's background as a theologian, before, during, and since the council, Father Thomas Guarino of the Immaculate Conception Seminary in South Orange, New Jersey (Archdiocese of Newark) offered this comment:

> It will mean, I suspect, a theologically nuanced and subtle
> pontificate, one greatly interested in continuing dialogue
> with the Orthodox and Protestant churches, and one that
> engages the great moral and bioethical issues of our day.
> Benedict XVI will probably continue to develop church
> teaching and practice, but it will be a development that
> is in fundamental continuity with the prior assertions
> of Scripture and tradition. He will also, I believe, defend
> human reason and rationality, and the human ability
> to attain truth, in the face of contemporary currents of
> relativism and postmodernism.[3]

Benedict the pope is Ratzinger the theologian, product of and participant in the greatest theological milestone in the history of the Catholic Church in the past five centuries.

"Co-worker of the Truth"

In the years after Vatican II, Ratzinger taught at the prestigious institutions in Munster and Tübingen, and published one of his greatest books, *Introduction to Christianity*. In 1969 he moved to the University of Regensburg, where he taught for the longest stretch in his academic career. That year, Pope Paul VI appointed him to the International Theological Commission. The drive to keep alive the spirit of the council animated Pope Paul VI and many of the bishops of Europe to implement the council's documents. The Theological Commission was seen as a potential counterweight to the Congregation for the Doctrine of the Faith, "or at least an opportunity to provide this Congregation with a new and wholly different 'brain trust,'" Ratzinger noted in his memoirs.

During this period, Ratzinger met another monumental figure of modern theology, Hans Urs von Balthasar, who became a great friend and ally in some of the tense debates in the commission. Meanwhile, his relationship with Karl Rahner became increasingly strained.

A significant event was the liturgical "revolution"—to which Ratzinger credits the publication of the *Missale Romanum* (Pope Paul's Missal, or liturgical text). While Ratzinger initially interpreted the Missal as a positive reform, he grew disappointed by its implementation by many priests and bishops, who, in Ratzinger's eyes, busied themselves with liturgical innovations that often went too far. He views liturgy, that is the practice of the rites of the church, such as Mass, as a tipping point in the history of the contemporary church—dating from the Reformation, when Protestants rejected many sacraments and ceremonies of the Catholic Church.

Ratzinger calls it a "confusing situation," and many Catholics would agree with that assessment. He has since called for a new liturgical movement to "call to life the real heritage of the Second Vatican Council." He views the "disintegration" of liturgy beginning in the 1970s as a crisis, and in his teaching career he came to focus on this aspect of the life of the church, which has carried into his time as a member of the Roman curia, and will no doubt be an important item on his agenda as Supreme Pontiff.

On March 24, 1977, nearly a dozen years after the conclusion of the council, Pope Paul VI appointed Father Joseph Ratzinger as archbishop of Munich and Freising. "I have loved my work as teacher and researcher. I certainly never aspired to head the administration of the Munich archdiocese. . . .It is a difficult task," Ratzinger told Messori. He was the first diocesan priest after eighty years to assume the pastoral responsibility of this large Bavarian diocese.

Today, the Archdiocese of Munich-Freising has a population of 1.9 million Catholics, about 60 percent of the total population. There are about 800 priests, 200 deacons, and 600 religious women and men serving 750 parishes. This compares, roughly to the Archdiocese of Los Angeles in the United States. The Diocese of Freising dates from 739, and the dual-city archdiocese from 1818.

Archbishop Ratzinger chose as his episcopal motto (which all bishops include on their coats of arms): *Cooperatores Veritatis*, or "Co-worker of the Truth" (from the third letter of St. John the Evangelist). Then, he was created a cardinal in the consistory of June 27, 1977, with four others, including Bernardin Gantin of Benin. A large contingent of the faithful from Munich were present in the Paul VI Audience Hall to witness his reception of the red biretta as a prince of the church.

Ratzinger's episcopal administration of Munich-Freising was marked by personal humility and willingness to work hard on administrative matters, to encourage priestly vocations, and to visit parishes throughout his archdiocese. He also spent a fair amount of time in Rome, attending to theological responsibilities.

One particular incident that emerged in the days after the election of Cardinal Ratzinger as Benedict XVI, reported by IANS (an online Indian news service), relates to a distant parish in Chungam, India. Father Abraham Kakkanattu, director of the Pushpagiri Medical College in Thiruvalla, helped to build the chapel of St. Mary Malankara Catholic Church in Chungam. Fundraising was difficult, and he looked for support from outside. Through an indirect connection he reached Archbishop Ratzinger in Munich in 1977 and submitted a detailed estimate of costs.

"Within a few days I received twenty thousand German marks with which I could build the church," Father Kakkanattu stated. The chapel became a full-fledged parish church, which bears Ratzinger's name on a marble memorial plaque.

Ratzinger went to Rome on an *ad limina* visit (as each bishop is required to do every five years), during the final year of Paul VI's pontificate. He was on holiday in Austria on August 6, 1978 when word came of Pope Paul's death. As a cardinal-elector, one of the youngest present, Ratzinger participated in both papal conclaves of 1978. He later said that he let himself be guided by providence in the choice. On August 26 of that year, Albino Luciani, Patriarch of Venice, was elected on the second day after only four ballots (exactly the number of ballots of the 2005 election).

He was on a trip to Ecuador, at a Marian conference in Guayaquil, when a local bishop informed him of Pope John Paul I's sudden, totally unexpected death. He has since supported the move toward beatification of John Paul I. He traveled to Rome for the October 16 election of Karol

Wojtyla, Archbishop of Krakow, as John Paul II, then returned to Munich to attend to business.

Quietly, methodically, doing much of the work behind the scenes, with the aid of auxiliary bishops, Joseph Ratzinger guided his flock during the late 1970s into the 1980s, but his tenure was destined to be short. Having declined an earlier invitation from his friend, John Paul II, Ratzinger later came to Rome in November 1981, after only four years as a residential archbishop—in a move that would change his life and fulfill his destiny as a theologian par excellence.

Twenty-three years after he resigned as archbishop, his election as pope received a mixed response in his native nation. In many places in Germany the church bells reportedly did not ring.

On April 20, 2005, the press quoted public opinion polls (as reported in the German news magazine *Der Spiegel*) that less than 30 percent of Germans responded favorably to Benedict's election, while more than 35 percent were opposed. In subsequent days, the numbers changed, rising to a 60-plus percent "approval rating" among his fellow countrymen.[4] "We consider the election of Ratzinger a catastrophe," said Bernd Goehring, a leader of the German Catholic ecumenical group Church from Below, as reported by Reuters. "It is very disappointing, even if it was predictable. We can expect no reform from him in the coming years."

CHAPTER 9

THE CONGREGATION

From November 25, 1981 to April 2, 2005, Cardinal Joseph Ratzinger served as prefect of the Sacred Congregation for the Doctrine of the Faith. His has been the longest tenure of a leader of a Vatican office in John Paul II's pontificate, indeed in the history of the church. His reputation as an enforcer of doctrine—which developed in a direction that surprised some colleagues—dates from these years. At John Paul's side, as perhaps his closest curial adviser, Ratzinger displayed the same qualities he had as a student and professor: ability to work long hours, interest in music, sophistication of thought and expression, and a deep holiness and dedication to prayer.

A Humble Worker in the Vineyard

Those who worked closely with him during this period describe a warm, humorous man, with a bottomless capacity to listen. His own publications (church documents, articles, books, and interviews) show his wide-ranging thought very clearly and often gracefully. He honed his language skills in Italian, Spanish, Portuguese, and English and largely ridded his speech of his native German accent when employing other spoken languages.

Among his fellow cardinals there was "always a deeply spiritual, quiet, kind pastor behind the pronouncements," according to Cindy Wooden of Catholic News Service. When he "put on his scholar's hat" in occasional public discussions and debates with fellow theologians, "there was no denying the twinkle in his eyes and the smile on his lips."[1]

However, from the point of view of liberal and progressive Catholics, including liberation theologians, feminist theologians, and many American Catholics, his near quarter century at the helm of the congregation was an unmitigated disaster, setting the church in "reverse," to a pre-Vatican II era of conformity, pessimism, lack of debate, and anti-modernity. It is not an exaggeration to describe the reaction of these Catholics to the news of Benedict's election as fearful and loathing. He was, and perhaps always will be, the "Panzer Cardinal" to them. American critics focus on the issues of sexual morality and contraception, homosexuality, priestly celibacy, and the ordination of women. This litmus test is not just a litany of complaint against the church's teaching, but also against the man who presented that teaching to the world as prefect of the congregation.[2]

Press coverage in the United States has emphasized the negative response to Ratzinger the enforcer of doctrine and to Benedict the "feared" pontiff. Hand-wringing among liberal pundits competes with barely concealed glee by traditional-minded clerics and conservative lay persons.

The response to his election from Jewish leaders, especially, was largely positive. For more than twenty years, the cardinal-prefect worked closely with John Paul II on opening their stance with Jews, increasing dialogue with other Christian communities, seeking forgiveness for past mistakes of the church and its members, and encouraging new ecclesial movements within the church. As prefect of the congregation Ratzinger often referred to the spirit and letter of Vatican II's openness to God's presence in faith traditions other than Catholic. Again, however, his critics found ample evidence, in their minds, of his closed-mindedness.

Thus, there is truly a chasm of understanding and acceptance of the man who now wears the Shoes of the Fisherman, St. Peter. However, knowing this does not seem to disturb the serenity of Pope Benedict, at least early on in his pontificate. Perhaps he became inured to it during those long, sometimes trying years in the Congregation for the Doctrine of the Faith. Over time, he is likely to mollify at least some of those who expressed displeasure at his election.

He called the prefecture his "so uncomfortable post, which at least allows me an overview of the general situation," and said, "inasmuch as I follow the reports which land on my desk every day, it has allowed me to grasp what concern for the universal Church means."[3] The Congregation for the Doctrine of the Faith was the first Vatican office to be reformed by Pope Paul VI, through a motu proprio on December 7, 1965, which confirmed its role of vigilance over matters of faith, but changed its procedures somewhat and changed its name from the Holy Office.

Previous to that, from its founding in 1542 by Pope Paul III, the office was called the Roman Inquisition and, as a commission of six cardinals, was charged to stem the spread of heresy (Protestantism) in northern Europe. Ratzinger went to great pains to separate the specific, and in his mind legitimate, task of the Roman Inquisition from the Spanish Inquisition, which was "in fact a tribunal of the Spanish king...created originally to try Jews and Mohammedans suspected of a 'feigned conversion' to a Catholicism which was also utilized by the crown as a political instrument."[4] Thus, it was sinful and illegitimate in its secular purpose and opposition to the popes.

During Ratzinger's historic tenure, the congregation saw two hugely important publications: the revised Code of Canon Law (in 1982) and the Catechism of the Catholic Church (various editions and languages throughout the later 1990s). These volumes will stand for the next half-century, at least, before the next revisions. A constant flow of questions, complaints, scandals, internal investigations, and prosecutions (such as the U.S. priests accused of sexual abuse) covered his desk. It was a crushing workload, and more than once he asked Pope John Paul II to relieve him, to allow him to retire, to appoint another, younger prelate to the post. But he labored on.

From the perspective of the congregation, orthodoxy is a hugely important, even precious commodity; faith is the highest good. Thus, making sure that religious and theological teaching are orthodox—adhere strictly to content of Catholic doctrine—is a task of great service, insuring the salvation of the teachers and the taught.

In the face of skepticism and outright rejection of the Catholic faith, Cardinal Ratzinger was convinced (and remains so, as pope) that there is, in fact, one truth and that its locus is in the church. Everything that he has written and taught since the early 1980s, including his pre-conclave homily to the cardinals on April 18, 2005, goes back to that central concept. Theology, then, in his experience as a teacher, and even more so as prefect of the congregation, is merely an expansion upon the core theme, a sometimes speculative treatment of finer points and practical, human, moral issues that arise in the world. Theology remains at the service of doctrine, which is at the service of the church, which is at the service of Jesus Christ. Revelation of the word and will of God—the basis of all doctrine—is found in Scripture, tradition, and the magisterium (the teaching authority of the church).

Doctrine and Dissent

In order to understand the man in his role as prefect of the congregation, it is appropriate to examine some of the statements and documents of the Congregation for the Doctrine of the Faith that he authored or supervised in the writing and promulgation. Ratzinger carried on a voluminous correspondence with bishops and internal correspondence within the Roman Curia, as well as giving interviews and theological talks throughout the world (mostly in Europe). He developed a view of the state of the church in the world, as well as its own structural integrity, that will inform his words and actions as pope in the wake of Vatican II and his powerful predecessor.

The themes and ongoing topics include moral teaching, the dignity and value of human life, and the promise of salvation for all mankind through Jesus Christ. What follows is a survey of some of the key texts from Ratzinger's congregation.

In September 2004, Pope John Paul II approved the congregation's publication of the "Letter to the Bishops of the Catholic Church on the Collaboration of Men and Women in the Church and in the World." In the letter the church blames the radical feminism of recent decades for causing "women [to believe that] in order to be themselves, [they] must make themselves adversaries of men." Such philosophy blurs the "difference or duality" of the sexes, demeans the woman as a human person, and stands in the way of her true liberation. Instead, the letter teaches the genders are distinct, and their relationship with one another must be based on love, equality, and reciprocity.

Cardinal Ratzinger's congregation called for an end to gender discrimination and the promotion of women in society; the letter supported women's right to work, if they choose: "Women should have access to positions of responsibility which allow them to inspire the policies of nations and to promote innovative solutions to economic and social problems."

When, in 2002 seven Catholic women were ordained as priests in a breakaway sect, the congregation issued a statement that reaffirmed John Paul's 1994 encyclical *Sacerdotis Ordinatio*, against the concept of the ordination of women: "The church has no authority to confer priestly ordination on women, that the Holy Father's teaching on the subject is to be believed by all the faithful."

Although not an official document, *Salt of the Earth: The Church at the End of the Century*, the cardinal's interview with German journalist Peter Seewald, who had written critically of the cardinal and the congregation, revealed Ratzinger's thinking. On the subject of the ordination of women, he says, "It is not…an infallible act of the pope, but the binding authority rests upon the continuity of the tradition. What the bishops teach and do in unison over a very long time is infallible."[5]

There was at least one instance of leaked correspondence, an official memorandum Cardinal Ratzinger sent to Cardinal Theodore E. McCarrick, archbishop of Washington, D.C. in July 2004 on the subject of abortion. The American prelate said that the text that reached public readers through an Italian newspaper was "an incomplete and partial leak" which did not reflect "the full message I received." Nonetheless, as Catholic News Service reported, it is clear that the memo outlined principles of moral and sacramental theology that should be taken into account in determining whether Catholic politicians who take policy positions contrary to church teaching should be allowed to receive Communion.[6] This was a hot button topic during the U.S. presidential elections in 2004.

In the document, Cardinal Ratzinger reaffirms the church's teaching that abortion and euthanasia are grave sins. The distinctions in moral theology between "formal" and "material" cooperation with evil (fine theological points for the vast majority of Catholics) are noted. For example, a Catholic office-seeker who consistently campaigns for and votes for permissive abortion laws is "formally" cooperating with evil. The congregation's leader reminds bishops that it is their responsibility to meet with an errant politician in such a case and instruct him in the teaching of the church and the norms for reception of the Eucharist.

One key passage hit home with Americans: "There may be a legitimate diversity of opinion even among Catholics about waging war and applying the death penalty, but not, however with regard to abortion and euthanasia."

In the October 1, 1986 "Letter to the Bishops of the Catholic Church on the Pastoral Care of Homosexual Persons," the cardinal acknowledges that "homosexuality and the moral evaluation of homosexual acts" have become a matter of public debate and should be addressed, "since this debate often advances arguments and makes assertions inconsistent with the teaching of the Catholic Church." He also cites a previous document, the "Declaration on Certain Questions Concerning Sexual Ethics," December 29, 1975.

One of the most controversial statements Cardinal Ratzinger ever made is contained in the 1986 letter. It is this sentence: "Although the particular inclination of the homosexual person is not a sin, it is a more or less strong tendency ordered toward an intrinsic moral evil; and thus the inclination itself must be seen as an objective disorder." He went on to condemn any form of violence or discrimination against homosexuals. Most importantly—the purpose of the letter—

he strongly encouraged more pastoral attention to be given to gay men and women.

As in other documents and statements, Cardinal Ratzinger claims biblical warrant and appeals to tradition in formulating a statement from the magisterium:

> The church's doctrine regarding this issue is thus based, not
> on isolated phrases for facile theological argument, but on
> the solid foundation of a constant biblical testimony....
> It is likewise essential to recognize that the Scriptures are
> not properly understood when they are interpreted in a way
> which contradicts the church's living Tradition. To be correct,
> the interpretation of Scripture must be in substantial accord
> with that Tradition.

This statement provides a key to understanding Ratzinger's entire theology.

The protection of human life was a frequent subject for Cardinal Ratzinger. On February 22, 1987, his office issued the "Instruction on Respect for Human Life in Its Origin and on the Dignity of Procreation." The congregation had been approached by bishops, theologians, and physicians to rule on bioethics, especially when it concerned reproduction, artificial or "test tube" conception, and the legitimacy of research using embryos or fetuses.

Bottom line: the Catholic Church does not and cannot condone any but "natural" method of conception of human life, and the use of the tissues of the unborn, especially when "harvested" for the purpose of research, is categorically wrong and sinful.

On the issues of ecumenical dialogue with non-Catholic Christian churches, the relation of the church to the Jews, and the relation of the church to other non-Christian religions and non-believers, the cardinal prefect of the congregation was engaged, along with his "boss," Pope John Paul, for the entire duration of his tenure. The quintessential document in this regard was the declaration *Dominus Jesus*, "On the Unicity and Salvific Universality of Jesus Christ and the Church," August 6, 2000, which is perhaps the most referred to and most quoted document from the congregation under his leadership. The declaration begins:

> The Lord Jesus, before ascending into heaven, commanded
> his disciples to proclaim the Gospel to the whole world and
> to baptize all nations: "Go into the whole world and proclaim
> the Gospel to every creature. He who believes and is baptized
> will be saved; he who does not believe will be condemned"
> (Mark 16:15–16).... The Church's universal mission is born
> from the command of Jesus Christ and is fulfilled in the
> course of the centuries in the proclamation of the mystery
> of God, Father, Son, and Holy Spirit, and the mystery of the
> incarnation of the Son, as saving event for all humanity.

The document calls for an open and positive approach, a "connection" with all other religious traditions in the world, citing Vatican II's Declaration on the Relation of the Church to Non-Christian Religions and calling for continued interreligious dialogue as part of the church's evangelizing mission. In an effort to support such dialogue, the document restates some of the fundamental truths that the magisterium has held: "to set forth again the doctrine of the Catholic faith in these areas, pointing out some fundamental questions that remain open to further development, and refuting specific positions that are erroneous or ambiguous."

The Ratzinger document is unequivocal in asserting "the definitive and complete character of the revelation of Jesus Christ," above and apart from the teaching of any other religion, and that the church of Jesus Christ subsists in the Catholic Church and the Catholic Church alone. These statements reflect "absolute truth and salvific universality" for Cardinal Ratzinger as the head of the doctrinal office and in his role as spokesman for the magisterium, the ultimate source of authority for such documents.

In words that sound stern, even harsh to some ears, the cardinal writes, "the obedience of faith implies acceptance of the truth of Christ's revelation, guaranteed by God, who is truth itself." Nonetheless, God makes himself available to people in religious traditions other than Catholic and other than Christian: "the salvific action of Jesus Christ, with and through his Spirit, extends beyond the visible boundaries of the church to all humanity." The historic schisms among Christian churches, however, makes it difficult to criticize while at the same time offering the olive branch of dialogue. This Ratzinger attempted to do.

The result? Initially, skeptics and critics focused on the negative interpretation of Ratzinger's words, then, over time, formed a better understanding and calmer acceptance (by some) of the terms of the debate as outlined in *Dominus Jesus*. For the cardinal, time often served as the salve that his words could not.

Perhaps more esoteric for many in advanced western democracies, but an urgent concern for John Paul and Cardinal Ratzinger early in the former's pontificate, was the concept of liberation theology as preached in poor nations, especially in Latin America, where people suffer from oppression under brutal authoritarian regimes, poverty, hunger, and sickness.

The "Instruction on Certain Aspects of the 'Theology of Liberation'" was published on August 6, 1984. In it, Ratzinger affirmed that "the Gospel of Jesus Christ is a message of freedom and a force for liberation." Further, he wrote, "liberation is first and foremost liberation from the radical slavery of sin. Its end and its goal is the freedom of the children of God." The position of the magisterium was that the Marxist critique of society is not and cannot be the basis for theological understanding and Christian action in the world. "Faced with the urgency of certain problems, some are tempted to emphasize, unilaterally, the liberation from servitude of an earthly and temporal kind." Liberation from sin then takes "second place" to political liberation from oppression.

The teaching of Jesus Christ is, according to the congregation, the most radical and the most complete "theology of liberation" available to mankind. Further, the pope decreed that Catholic priests could not hold political office at any level in any country, even for the "right reasons." Their calling, and that of the church, remains above the temporal and secular concerns, of even the most desperate among the oppressed.

A huge issue within the governance of the Catholic Church is that of collegiality among the bishops of the church. Another way of stating it is that some—perhaps many—bishops around the world see the centralization of authority of the Holy See, rather than the more or less equal sharing of authority among the local churches (dioceses), as destructive to the ultimate mission of the church, to carry the gospel of Jesus Christ. The bishops themselves, as individuals and in national and regional conferences, have seen a decrease in their autonomy, a looming presence of "Rome" in their backyards.

Even a brother German bishop and cardinal expressed disagreement with Ratzinger on this trend, and posed some other questions. Cardinal Walter Kasper, president of the Pontifical Council for Promoting Christian Unity and former bishop of Rottenburg-Stuttgart, Germany, spoke out in 2001, stating in the U.S. magazine *America* (April 23–30) and the British Catholic periodical *The Tablet* (June 23): "The bishop is not a delegate of the pope but rather a representative of Jesus Christ: he enjoys his own sacramentally based individual responsibility."

In his response published in *America* (November 19, 2001), Cardinal Ratzinger referred to his congregation's June 28, 1992 "Letter to the Bishops of the Catholic Church on Some Aspects of the Church as Communio." In that document he wrote of the principle "that the universal church (*ecclesia universalis*) is in its essential mystery a reality that takes precedence, ontologically and temporally, over the individual local churches."

Kasper shot back in a German newspaper: "The formula becomes thoroughly problematic if the universal church is being covertly identified with the church of Rome, and de facto with the pope and the curia. If that happens, the letter from the Congregation for the Doctrine of the Faith cannot be read as an aid in clarifying communion ecclesiology, but as a dismissal of it and as an attempt to restore Roman centralism." Ratzinger agreed with Kasper's "clarification" but wondered "why does this same association [that is, equating "universal church" with "pope and curia"] keep coming up everywhere, even with so great a theologian as Walter Kasper? What makes people suspect that the thesis of the internal priority of the one divine idea of the church over the individual churches might be a ploy of Roman centralism?"

CARDINAL RATZINGER'S WRITINGS

Pope Benedict XVI has been a prolific writer. To date, he has authored, coauthored, or edited more than sixty books. Here is a partial bibliography of his major works.

* *Introduction to Christianity* (1968, 2000)
* *God of Jesus Christ* (1978)
* *The Ratzinger Report: An Exclusive Interview on the State of the Church* (1985)
* *Feast of Faith: Approaches to a Theology of the Liturgy* (1986)
* *Principles of Christian Morality* (1986)
* *Principles of Catholic Theology: Building Stones for a Fundamental Theology* (1987)
* *"In the Beginning...": A Catholic Understanding of the Story of Creation and the Fall* (1990, 1995)
* *Eschatology—Death and Eternal Life* (1989)
* *To Look on Christ: Exercises in Faith, Hope, and Love* (1991)
* *Co-Workers of the Truth: Meditations for Every Day of the Year* (1992)
* *The Meaning of Christian Brotherhood* (1993)
* *A Turning Point for Europe?: The Church in the Modern World— Assessment and Forecast* (1994)
* *The Nature and Mission of Theology: Essays to Orient Theology in Today's Debates* (1995)
* *Called to Communion: Understanding the Church Today* (1996)
* *Salt of the Earth: The Church at the End of the Millennium: An Interview with Peter Seewald* (1997)
* *Catechism of the Catholic Church: Corrigenda* (1998)
* Ad Tuendam Fidem—*To Protect the Faith* (1998)
* *Milestones: Memoirs 1927-1977* (1998)
* *Many Religions, One Covenant: Israel, the Church, and the World* (1999)
* *The Spirit of the Liturgy* (2000)
* Dominus Iesus: *The Lord Jesus* (2000)
* *God and the World: A Conversation with Peter Seewald* (2002)
* *God Is Near Us: The Eucharist, the Heart of Life* (2003)
* *Truth and Tolerance: Christian Belief and World Religions* (2004)
* *Pilgrim Fellowship of Faith: The Church As Communion* (2005)

So continues the theological debates among cardinals. However, now Cardinal Kasper, who voted in the conclave that elected Benedict XVI, will not be on a level playing field with his "opponent."

Measure of the Man

Much of the work of the Congregation for the Doctrine of the Faith was, and always has been, carried on behind closed doors. A shadow of sorts hangs over the office since it is responsible for silencing or removing theologians whose teaching and writing is deemed contrary to Catholic doctrine, such as Charles Curran and Roger Haight, who can no longer teach Catholic theology at Catholic institutions. However, Ratzinger the person has been credited by supporters and some of his critics alike as being moderately open, meeting with critics (within and outside of the church), and listening. Journalists have found him engaging and "good copy." He engages in public debates (as with Cardinal Kasper and others)—even seems to enjoy it.

Above all, by those who have spent time with him, he is universally described as a keen listener.

Why, then, the reputation as a somber, pessimistic "enforcer"? Certainly the demeanor of the curial powerhouse that the world had known up until his election as pope was rather stern. The nature of his work, too, required a seriousness in expression that could fairly be called portentous. And his unabashed certainty about the content of the faith chilled those with relativistic tendencies to the bone.

And it seems from biographical sources that though his personal optimism and faith in Jesus Christ survived Nazism and world war, as well as the academic and theological "wars" of his early priesthood, the worldwide phenomena of relativism, secularism, and hedonism, as evidenced in student unrest in the late 1960s (right outside his own window) and the drug and sexual revolutions of the same time, changed him. He saw the world—and many within the Catholic Church itself—as rejecting the Gospel. He must have wondered: How could this be when Christ offered such a beautiful alternative to evil and selfishness? How could anyone who had heard the teaching not believe it with all his heart and mind? How could Catholics question the long-established, brilliantly expressed teachings on morality, faith, and salvation?

Thorough scholarly research and clear, forceful writing about the truth were not enough to convert the world. For the world has not yet—and perhaps cannot ever—accept the one eternal truth, as presented by the Roman Catholic Church, whole and unsweetened. That is the fate of the "watchdog," to warn of imminent danger and to stand ready to defend his master.

Joseph Ratzinger confronts a different fate, a different task, upon his election as pope. He turns from admonisher-in-chief to shepherd of the flock. Like his predecessor it is unlikely that he will put down his pen. It is so much a part of who he is. But he has, in addition, taken up the shepherd's staff, the crosier of the bishop of Rome. He assumed the pallium, the lamb's wool stole of the metropolitan archbishop, upon his installation on April 24, 2005, as symbol of the universal jurisdiction he now holds. He wore the vestments that had been created for John Paul II and put on the Ring of the Fisherman that the successors of St. Peter have worn for centuries uncounted. At that event, attended by an estimated 350,000 people, including many from his native Bavaria as well as delegations from more than 130 nations, he proclaimed, boldly and simply, "The church is alive!" He now faces a new era, a new and different responsibility for an old and certain man.

If history teaches us anything about ourselves, as human beings and as individuals, it is that we become who we already are—that our parentage and childhood, our growing up and going out, our finding and staying, our maturity and eventual passing, are written anew each day with words both strange and familiar. For Joseph Ratzinger, Pope Benedict XVI, his is an exceptional history of which many more volumes are yet to be written.

CHAPTER 10

URBI ET ORBI:
THE STATE OF THE CHURCH
IN THE WORLD

The shock and jubilation of the papal election is over. The pageantry of the Holy Father's installation (scaled back a generation ago from the medieval tradition of papal "coronation") is finished. Pope Benedict XVI must now turn to the business of the apostolic office to which he was elected. And, in a world of instant communication that often reels from tragedy to tragedy, there is no time to waste.

The new pope will confront a myriad of issues, spiritual and temporal, pastoral and political, administrative and structural. He will place each decision that he makes within the context of church teaching and history, while at the same time being (or becoming) aware of the exigencies of the contemporary world. This is no easy task, to say the least. It will take an extraordinary amount of will, intellect, focus, and deep spirituality simply to get through the daily demands and responsibilities that confront a world leader such as the Holy Father, who is responsible for about one billion souls.

There are schools of nearly equal vehemence that declare either that the Catholic Church is in an inevitable and irreversible decline, or that the church has entered a new, albeit painful phase of renewal and rebirth. The new pope cannot afford to believe, nor does he in fact subscribe to the former position. It would be defeatist and irresponsible of him to do so. It would also be inaccurate, as the church continues to grow rapidly in many parts of the world, especially in what was once called the "Third World." Yet, can the pope truly believe in and represent an optimistic position for his church in the face of disappointing, sinful, and damaging events that have battered and beleaguered the church for more than a half-century?

In fact, the sweeping and even devastating changes in the church and the world during our day are little different from (indeed, less threatening than) those of other historical eras, times of persecution, barbarian invasion, heresies, schisms, and devastating plagues. If one looks back at the beginning of any recent pontificate, even going back as far as a century or two, one will see this combination of missionary success and internal uncertainty. As Pope John XXIII spoke in 1962, on the first day of the gathering of the world's bishops for the Second Ecumenical Council of the Vatican:

> We are shocked to discover what is being said by some
> people who, though they may be fired by religious zeal,
> are without justice, or good judgment, or consideration
> in their way of looking at matters. In the existing state of
> society they see nothing but ruin and calamity. They are
> in the habit of saying that our age is much worse than past
> centuries. They behave as though history, which teaches us
> about life, has nothing to teach them. ...On the contrary,
> we should recognize that, at the present historical moment,
> Divine Providence is leading us towards a new order in

human relationships which, through the agency of man
and what is more above and beyond their own expectations,
are tending towards the fulfillment of higher and, as yet,
mysterious and unforeseen designs.[1]

Pope John's speech "was rightly seen as an incitement to action and an optimistic acceptance of change," wrote Paul Johnson in *A History of Christianity*.[2] Doom and disaster have ever been around the corner for the world and the church, and both have endured and evolved.

John's *aggiornamento* ("updating") of the Catholic Church did not mean that doctrine would change in any way, but that the ways in which church teachings were presented would be adapted to the contemporary world and to diverse cultures and situations. It was also a way to invigorate the stodgy triumphalist and negative aura in which the hierarchy seemed trapped at that time. He was elected at an advanced age and reigned for less than five years, but the church turned in a new direction because of him. But, inevitably, especially in just the past few years there has been a clear move back toward uniformity of liturgical practices, for example, which, while it does not reverse the innovations of Vatican II, turns the clock back a few hours.

So, the new pope takes center stage as a decades—and centuries—old drama continues to unfold.

Transition

One of the first challenges Pope Benedict XVI faces is the transition from his immediate predecessor, one of the longest-serving popes in the history of the church. Even during the long twilight of John Paul's pontificate when he was crippled with physical ailments, he remained almost frenetically active, canonizing and beatifying dozens of men and women, traveling to Cuba, Ukraine, Canada, and Poland, among other places, and promulgating encyclicals and homilies on the rosary and the nature of the papacy itself.

Upon his election in 1978, John Paul II had kept the cardinal-electors in conclave for an extra day, celebrated mass the next morning, and announced to the electors that his first task was to complete the implementation of the Second Vatican Council, especially the document *Lumen gentium*, the Dogmatic Constitution on the Church, which he called a "Magna Carta." The newly elected pope will face immediate comparison to John Paul II's strategic brilliance and personal charisma—and he will be expected by all parties to deal with the lingering aftershock of Vatican II. Benedict is exceptionally well-equipped for the latter challenge.

Despite the enormous upheavals and changes within the church over the past forty years since the Second Vatican Council (1962–65), the work of the council is not yet completely implemented, and the spirit of the council is not yet fully accepted by the universal church. In the U.S. and abroad, there are movements to return to the Latin mass and to diminish lay involvement in liturgy and local governance. Of late—that is, over the past decade or longer—the more conservative interpretation of the council, that it was not a "revolution" as many have described it, has gained currency in theological circles.

Further, it generally takes decades, even centuries, for the full effect of an ecumenical council of the church—which is a gathering of all the bishops of the world at the behest of the pope to debate and resolve problems or crises—to be felt. Three centuries passed between the Council of Trent (1545–63) and the First Vatican Council

(1869–70), and nearly a hundred passed between the most recent two councils.

The new pope was not a bishop at Vatican II, as his four immediate predecessors were: Bl. John XXIII, who convoked the council; Paul VI, who held it together and continued the council through the latter three sessions; John Paul I, a relatively young bishop in those years; and John Paul II, a very young Polish auxiliary bishop whose voice was heard and respected by his elder council fathers and who became Archbishop of Krakow during the council. However, as a *peritus* and an important interpreter of council documents, Joseph Ratzinger has "lived" the council uniquely and fully.

Pope John Paul II very consciously, and conscientiously, placed himself in the footsteps of Paul VI with regards to the implementation of the council's documents on liturgy, bishops, laity, ecumenism, the Blessed Virgin Mary, relations with non-Christians, relations with the orthodox churches, and others. At the same time, the late pontiff and the magisterium of the church understood and promoted the notion that Vatican II was a continuation of the rather icy and abortive First Ecumenical Council of the Vatican under Pius IX, which is most famous for the controversial (even then) definition of papal infallibility.

What will happen? Will the new pope wish to revive the spirit of openness and diversity that blew through St. Peter's Basilica during those crucial years of renewal? Or will this newly elected Roman Pontiff continue on the path toward ever-increasing bureaucratic centralization of ecclesiastical governance, weakening the influence and autonomy of regional bishops' conferences?

Catholics will watch with interest and listen for signals from the 263rd pope. As an experienced curial administrator he will most likely tack cautiously back toward the safer shore of more centralization, while avoiding monarchic trappings and the "ultramontanism" (the absolute, inflexible authority of the pope) of the nineteenth century that still appeals to some within the hierarchy and the Roman Curia.

Morality

The Roman Pontiff is considered the universal pastor of the church, and as such, its leading moral teacher. No pope can escape, nor would he wish to, this responsibility, but each emphasizes what is most important to him and most necessary to the time. When he speaks *ex cathedra* on issues of faith and morals, he is considered infallible. This occurs when he has consulted with the college of bishops, his magisterium, and pronounces on church dogma in a definitive way. The last time a pope spoke in this way was a half-century ago when Pius XII promulgated the dogma of the Ascension of the Blessed Virgin Mary.

But the pope speaks out often and definitively on issues regarding life, marriage, sexuality, and right and wrong behavior. The specter of Paul VI's encyclical on human reproduction and contraception, *Humanae vitae*—which reinforced the church's traditional views on these subjects—continues to loom over any discussion of sexual morality and marriage in the Roman Catholic Church. Since its promulgation in 1968, there has been a continuous discussion of this teaching, and the orthodox position has gained strength within the church, while its impact on the non-Catholic world has been felt in debates over gay marriage, for example. Compassion for AIDS sufferers, victimized children, single mothers, and broken families remains a core teaching in the spirit of the gospel virtue of love for one's neighbor and charity for those in need. All that said, it is unlikely that church teaching on artificial contraception will change.

What will happen? Preaching on moral issues is one of the pope's most important duties, and this pope has forcefully spoken and written on the subject for decades. Some have already called on him to "modify" his strict moral positions. Time may not be on his side, though. The example of John XXIII is illustrative in this respect: he wasted no time, perhaps because he was elderly and in poor health for much of his brief pontificate. Pope Benedict will probably issue a major encyclical letter or other major document within the first few months of his reign. The world will be waiting.

Pope Benedict will continue the church's strong opposition to abortion and to capital punishment, which so marked John Paul II's pontificate as he preached against what he called the "culture of death" which he found pervasive in the world. The catch-all term "life" will remain the key word in the pope's teaching in this area: the church will not and theologically cannot reverse or even amend its policies on abortion, fetal stem cell research, euthanasia, and capital punishment.

On the related issue of bioethics, Benedict helped to formulate the position and to author Vatican statements on this sensitive issue, including the strong, irreversible stand against embryonic stem cell research. There simply is no more staunch pro-life advocate in the church than Joseph Ratzinger has been and will continue to be.

Secularization

As part of his moral worldview and regional political considerations, Pope John Paul II's curia was focused, with Cardinal Ratzinger's involvement, on amending the European constitution to acknowledge the foundational role of Christianity in the history and culture of the continent. This effort is unlikely to succeed because of Europe's sharp turn to secularization in all phases of life and culture. Numerous surveys taken over the past two decades have shown that church attendance in Europe is the lowest in the entire world—this at the heart of what was once called Christendom! By contrast, American church attendance is far less anemic.

For the pope, secularization is a major concern at the outset of his pontificate, a nagging, gnawing "enemy" of the church: the drive by cultural and political forces to remove religion from public discourse. This is in reaction to centuries of church influence, most especially in European politics—and in the U.S. it is fueled by civil libertarians who promote the notion of diversity of religious belief, and non-belief, in our society. In France, the government has explicitly prohibited religious clothing or symbols of any faith to be worn in the classroom. Civil unions in the U.S. are supported for gay couples, to sanction relationships outside the sacralized institution of marriage.

What will happen? The culture wars will continue, both in the U.S. and in Europe, especially. The war on terrorism injects religiosity into the public arena in a different way, causing secular governments and non-religious believers to appeal to "sensitivity" regarding treatment of Muslims in their own countries and throughout the world. The cardinals' choice of the German Ratzinger means they have not "written off" Europe.

The best the Holy Father can do is to follow the lead of John Paul II and remain consistent in his critique of and his engagement with secular leaders and governments. Here, the pope's role as head of state of a sovereign nation comes into play. He has the opportunity to meet face-to-face with political leaders, with ambassadors, and with cultural figures—as much or as little as he cares to.

Ecumenism and Relations with Jews

The reformers within the church at large, and within the colleges of bishops and cardinals, look to ecumenism, that is, dialogue and closer relationships with non-Catholic Christian churches, as one of the highest priorities that emerged from Vatican II. Not all church leaders agree; in fact, the curial leadership has been divided, with a bias toward less openness to ecumenical initiatives and a somewhat grudging acceptance of efforts currently under way.

Dr. Rowan Williams, the Archbishop of Canterbury and leader of the Anglican Communion, met with John Paul II in November 2003, but no substantive new developments were expected in relations between the Anglican and Catholic communions. The major reason for the stalled talks was the ordination of an openly gay bishop by the Episcopal Church of the United States. That event caused not only a potential schism within the American branch of Anglicanism but among other international branches. The ordination of female priests and bishops had already caused increased tensions between the Anglican and Catholic Churches; the Catholic Church will not accept the ordination of women as priests or openly gay clergy.

A pet project of sorts for John Paul was the attempt to bring the Eastern Orthodox churches and the Latin church of Rome into a closer relationship. Since 1054 the two branches of Christianity have been separated and oftentimes bitterly adversarial. Theological, cultural, and political differences have kept the two at arm's length for nearly a millennium, despite the desire of numerous popes and councils to achieve reunion.

John Paul II reached out to various representatives of orthodoxy and likely would have convoked a new ecumenical council—Vatican III?—if he thought reunion was a serious possibility. In 2002 he apologized to the patriarch of Constantinople for past sins of the Catholic Church toward the East; and the apology was accepted in 2004! The Russian Orthodox Church in particular has pointedly criticized the Roman Church for attempting to proselytize, trying to usurp the traditional predominance of orthodoxy in the post-Soviet Russia.

What will happen? Ecumenism offers both opportunity and high risk for the pope. Yet he cannot completely put it on the back burner; too much time and effort have been invested since Vatican II, and the faithful around the world expect the Vatican to lead the way in ongoing efforts to bring the "separated brethren" and "Holy Mother Church" back together. In his early homilies and messages Benedict has indicated a genuine interest in ecumenical dialogue.

Thus, he cannot "lose" by making ecumenism and relations with non-Christians a priority of his pontificate. In a world so bitterly divided along religious and cultural and political lines—with dangerous chasms between Muslims and Christians, for example—billions of people will pay attention to anything that Pope Benedict XVI does to continue ecumenical and inter-religious dialogue. He will be expected to continue John Paul II's masterful gestures of unity and reconciliation (such as meeting frequently with leading rabbis and seeking opportunities to meet with Orthodox and Protestant leadership).

In fact, perhaps the greatest progress and one of John Paul's greatest legacies could be identified in the area of Jewish-Catholic relations. The new pope has succeeded a daunting example of a natural bridge-builder (the meaning of the Latin word "pontifex") in this crucial aspect of the modern papacy. No one, from this time forward, will be able to do less and expect the approbation of Christians and Jews who desire true reconciliation between the faiths. As a cardinal, Benedict was certainly on board with John Paul.

Jews and Catholics have achieved much common ground, despite extremists in both communities who would wish otherwise. The momentum will not be lost if the new pontiff is willing and conscientious about continuing the dialogue. In addition, the pontiff must be prepared to respond to incidents of anti-Semitism throughout the world, as a practical demonstration of the church's position on this issue.

War and Terrorism

The dawn of the third Christian millennium has seen religious and ideologically based terrorism on a global scale never before experienced in modern times (say, for the past century). Despite the ongoing dialogue between the Catholic Church and Muslims, attempting to find common religious grounds to promote co-existence, extremists in both camps are distrustful, even hateful, of the other.

Jews, too, have a stake in this conflict that always directly affects the very existence of the state of Israel. The Holy See, has been more concerned with religious dialogue than political security for Israel; however, the pope's men are conscious of the needs of the tiny minority of Christians in the Holy Land, about two percent of the total current population. Remember that in 2002 gunmen took over the Church of the Nativity in Bethlehem during a time of violence between the Israeli army and Palestinians—possibly presaging future incidents.

Further, the Holy See opposed the U.S. invasion of Iraq in March 2003 (again, Ratzinger was in sync with the pope on the issue). This position was welcomed by those Americans who opposed what they saw as preemptive and unilateral military action against a nation that was not an imminent threat to the United States. It displeased Americans who supported the war as necessary and justified, and it put U.S. churchmen in an awkward position—not for the first time—vis a vis the pope.

The United Nations organization is no friend of the pope and the Catholic Church (due to public clashes in the past on issues of birth control and abortion) but remains possibly the only international venue where the pope can engage the issues of war and terrorism on a global basis. He uses his general audiences and homilies, as well as formal documents (encyclicals), to present his gospel-centered pleas for peace among all men. But he can only be a moral voice in the struggle, for he is powerless to bring military or political pressure to bear on any side in a deadly conflict.

This is the way of the contemporary world, the reality for the past four centuries, which is very different than the medieval papacy that wielded troops as well as indulgences in Europe and the Middle East.

What will happen? Confronting issues of war and peace is what a pope does, what popes have done for two millennia. This one will look to Benedict XV's example during World War I and Pope Pius XII's example during World War II, as well as John XXIII's and Paul VI's Cold War and Vietnam War statements. The Roman church nearly always seeks to build on papal precedents as well as scripture—and nearly always promotes peace over any other option available, even morally justifiable military action.

This Pope Benedict will seek every moral and diplomatic way to bring about peace between combatants and probably will continue the Vatican's tenuous tilt against the Israeli government's strong security policies.

The Church in the United States

Regarding the American Catholic Church, any pope must deal with this unique body of believers, which numbers more than 65 million and continues to grow.[3] This is not to say that other regional and national church groups are not also unique, but the U.S. church is a particular thorn in the side of any pontiff, due to its size and its wealth. And since the spring of 2002, when the long-suppressed clergy child abuse scandal rocketed into the headlines across the nation, the American church has been in crisis.

The bishops sought the Vatican's approval to institute new norms and procedures to deal with this ugly issue, which they received. Recently, the United States Conference of Catholic Bishops released the results of an audit of each of the 194 dioceses in the country and a survey-history of the problem over the past fifty years. It is, at best, a mixed picture: dioceses have taken steps, some of them more effectively than others, to root out the problem and to protect children now and in the future. The bishops seem to have broken through the shame and denial that kept the problem under wraps for so long. But the faithful in the church still must work through the shock and disappointment surrounding how criminal clergy members and their victims were dealt with over the past five decades.

Cardinal Ratzinger, as prefect of a key office, was in the forefront of the investigations and decisions regarding priests found guilty of abuse. He reopened the investigation into long-standing allegations against a prominent Mexican priest in December 2004.

Apart from this current scandal and crisis, the rank and file within the American church maintains a tenuous, frequently suspicious, sometimes problematic relationship with Rome. Again, reaching back to the Second

Vatican Council and the 1960s, the fault line has not been overcome between American Catholics focused on "reform" and the forces of orthodoxy within the American hierarchy and the Roman Curia. Mistrust over decades of a back-and-forth tussle between so-called liberal and conservative sides—with extreme proponents on each end of the spectrum—has created a lasting tension within the American church and between it and the Vatican. Examples include debate over Vatican II liturgical reforms, academic freedom in Catholic universities, the role of women (with emphasis on the ordination of women as priests), and the obligation of Catholic politicians to "be Catholic" in the public arena.

What will happen? The new pope faces a hornet's nest of issues in the Holy See's relationship with the American Catholic Church, but retains, as always, the upper hand in terms of dogma and discipline. The American cardinals and bishops will follow his lead, albeit sometimes reluctantly. (Note in Chapter 9 the leaked 2004 memo to Cardinal McCarrick as an example of his previous dealings with U.S. prelates.)

The American church will remain a bellwether as well as an anomaly in the Catholic world. As the bishops struggle to resolve the clergy-sex abuse scandal, they will try to refocus on issues of social justice and life (being anti-abortion, anti-death penalty, and anti-embryonic stem cell research). Pope Benedict may visit the United States at his earliest opportunity to reaffirm his authority over and crucial interest in the American church.

Persecution of the Church

Nearly three hundred Catholics were "martyred" in 2003, according to the Vatican.[4] That is, they were killed because they witnessed to their faith in Jesus Christ. Repressive regimes such as China, political violence in central and southern Asia, Muslim-on-Christian violence such as in Africa, and rebellions in Latin America all claimed the lives of Catholic clergy, religious, and laity. Arguably, this represents a new wave of worldwide persecutions of Catholics.

John Paul decried this violence against the faithful, emphasizing modern martyrs among the many saints he has canonized over the past quarter century. He worked behind the scenes through diplomatic and non-official channels to support endangered churches and Catholics. His elevation of the archbishop of Khartoum, Sudan, for example, highlighted the dire situation of the Catholic minority in that country and perhaps saved some lives by focusing the world's attention on the dangers there. However, John Paul's final spiritual testament did not reveal the name of the cardinal he named "in pectore," or close to the heart, in 2003. This practice is generally an effort to protect a cardinal from harassment by an oppressive regime.

What will happen? The new pope will need to deal somehow with such persecutions as a threat to the universal church as well as individual bishops in their dioceses. He has at his disposal the diplomatic resources of the Secretariat of State, as well as the goodwill of faithful Catholics and friendly governments throughout the world.

But there are enemies, too, who oppose the church and everything it stands for. As with war and terrorism, the Holy Father will attempt to walk a delicate public tightrope, but privately he will probably pull out all stops to support and protect those who face the threat or reality of persecution. He faces the same problem that wartime popes, especially Cold War popes, confronted for decades, but with a less coherent opponent. This time it is not a Roman Empire or a Soviet Communist bloc, but rather individual states and religious factions that threaten the well-being of Catholics in spots all over the globe. It is an intractable problem that can be tackled only with focus and discipline and diplomatic competence.

Priestly Celibacy and the Role of Women

Catholics throughout the world do not expend as much intellectual energy as Americans and/or Western Europeans do on issues of priestly celibacy and the potential ordination of women as priests or deacons. The new pope will eventually have to acknowledge the theological arguments that have been raised since Vatican II in the more "progressive" sectors of the Catholic Church, as did Pope John Paul II. Though over the course of the previous pontificate, as John Paul's chief doctrinal "enforcer," Cardinal Joseph Ratzinger became seemingly less and less open to theological development in this area and more interested in maintaining the status quo: liberation and feminist theologies took a decided back pew in that regime.

What will happen? It is likely that nothing will happen over the next decade or so, in this pontificate or the next, regarding the thousand-year-old discipline of celibacy for Roman Catholic priests. The anticipated shortage of priests will come to a crisis point, probably, in about 2025, in the U.S. and elsewhere (it already exists in some dioceses here and in pockets around the world). But the Holy See does not count that, in itself, as a strong enough argument to reconsider married or female priests.

Unless there is another ecumenical council of the church (an unlikely "Vatican III"—if Cardinal Ratzinger's own firm statements are to be believed), the problem will remain on the pope's back burner. Period.

Governance and Collegiality

The Church teaches that the Holy Father possesses the fullness of authority—spiritual, juridical, temporal—invested in St. Peter, to whom Jesus Christ gave the keys of the kingdom, the power to "bind and loose" human sin. This is no fantasy or metaphor for believers, but the rock-solid foundation of Catholics' professed faith in the one, holy, and apostolic church. The church is "one" because it is unified and universal, as intended by Christ; it is "holy" because it is of God, founded, blessed, and sustained by his grace, through the Holy Spirit. It is "apostolic" because it was handed down directly by the apostles, the divinely chosen leaders of the early church. Any man who accepts election as Peter's successor, then, places himself in this line of apostolic authority. He is bound to believe it and to teach it, as it has been preserved in the deposit of faith and passed down to him.

How a pope wields this authority, how he interprets and delegates this authority, is what matters in a practical sense. The issue of collegiality, touched on in Chapter 9, is a lingering one that all popes have confronted, especially during and since the Second Vatican Council. The approximately 4,000 bishops of the world function as a "college," that is a fraternal body of peers and advisers to the pope, though rarely (if ever) do they act as a body and with anything approaching unanimity. The pope personally appoints each bishop through the Congregation for Bishops, and each bishop takes a pledge of loyalty to the pope as head of the College of Bishops. It is an intimate relationship but always at arm's length. There are national, regional, ethnic, and theological differences that divide the bishops themselves; the late pope attempted to rein in and unify the world's bishops under his "universal jurisdiction" as Supreme Pontiff. Only a handful of American bishops remain in place who were appointed by John Paul's predecessor.

Pope John Paul I gave every indication in his brief, thirty-three-day reign that his would be a humbler, more collegial exercise of papal authority than most who had come before. His successor, John Paul II, seized upon virtually every opportunity to demonstrate the power, validity, and contemporary relevance of the papal office, often to the astonishment of the watching world. The seismic effect of his trips to his native Poland, as pilgrim and as Supreme Pontiff, offer but one example in proof of his stage presence, personal popularity, and formidable communication skill in service of papal power.

What will happen? It is likely that the new pontiff will have to navigate a middle course between a traditional monarchical and a post-Vatican II collegial exercise of his office. Vatican II began a process of quasi-"democratization" or modest liberalization of church governance with its emphasis on collegiality and cooperation among the bishops. However, all the while, the authority of the pope remained unchallenged, even enhanced in the aftermath of Vatican I and the documents on church and bishops. And, most importantly, the Holy Father retains the canonical right to name each and every bishop in the world, thus putting his stamp on the hierarchy and creating the most lasting legacy of any pontificate.

It seems inevitable that Pope Benedict will reach out to the world's Catholic bishops within a year or so of his election, holding the Synod of Bishops scheduled for autumn 2005. He will depend upon the bishops to execute his "marching orders" for Catholics worldwide but, like his predecessors, will encounter conflicts with individuals and national groups along the way. He may re-empower the national bishops' conferences, which the previous pontificate downplayed, even disenfranchised to a large degree.

Pope Benedict will need to appoint bishops in at least a couple dozen key dioceses very soon. These choices will be telling—they will reveal how he works with the curial bureaucracy and the type of episcopal leader he wants in position in the dioceses around the world.

These are just some of the most crucial items on the agenda of Pope Benecict XVI's church, at least those that he inherits upon assuming the office of Vicar of Christ. He may introduce others, based on his personal experiences and preferences—and no doubt there will be new crises and problems that time has yet to reveal. Upon his election, he and the cardinal-electors knew the incredible burden that he assumed when he uttered the simple word "Accepto. I accept." He now trusts those same cardinals to assist him, and the Holy Spirit to guide him to the right decisions for the church he has vowed to lead.

THE CHRONOLOGY OF THE POPES AND THE PAPACY

ach entry in the chronology below is numbered, with the papal name and pontificate dates provided. Following each pope's birth name (when applicable), nationality, and birth date (when available), is a brief note on the significant aspects of his pontificate.

An **asterisk** indicates abdication, resignation, deposition, or assassination of a pope (excluding martyrdom for the faith, documented and traditional). When available, the date of death is provided.

St. = Canonized a saint
Bl. = Proclaimed blessed

1. ST. PETER THE APOSTLE   died circa A.D. 64 or 67
Simon Bar-Jonah, Judean. Acknowledged as a principal leader among the original Twelve Apostles and in the young church after Pentecost.

2. ST. LINUS   circa 66–78
Possibly Italian. Status based largely on the list made by St. Irenaeus of Lyons of the first twelve successors of Peter, written in about A.D. 180.

3. ST. ANACLETUS [CLETUS]   circa 78–88
Possibly a former Greek slave. Name means "blameless"; possibly appointed or chaired a council of fellow presbyters in Rome.

4. ST. CLEMENT I   circa 88–97
Possibly Roman. Putative author of the Letter to Corinthians (circa 96) as chief correspondent or presider of the church of Rome.

5. ST. EVARISTUS   circa 97–105
Greek. Credited (perhaps erroneously) with dividing Rome into parishes and naming seven deacons to assist the pope while he preached and to substantiate his orthodoxy.

6. ST. ALEXANDER I   circa 105–115
Possibly Roman. According to J.N.D. Kelly in *Oxford Dictionary of Popes*: "Virtually nothing is reliably known about him except that he held a leading position in the Roman church."

7. ST. SIXTUS I   circa 115–125
Greek or Roman. Possibly a martyr.

8. St. Telesphorus   circa 125–136
Greek. The only second-century pope whose martyrdom is documented.

9. St. Hyginus   circa 136–140
Greek. Little is known of his reign, except that he was the eighth successor of Peter according to St. Irenaeus's list.

10. St. Pius I   circa 140–155
Possibly Italian. Consolidation of authority in a single bishop—the monoepiscopal form of church governance that exists today—began about this time, under Pius's reign.

11. St. Anicetus   circa 155–166
First of six Syrian popes. Denied the request of St. Polycarp that Easter be celebrated on the fourteenth of Nisan, sparking Quartodeciman controversy.

12. St. Soter   circa 166–175
Italian. Established Easter as annual liturgical celebration and continued consolidation of papal authority over churches throughout the world.

13. St. Eleutherius   circa 175–189
Greek. Had been deacon to Pope Anicetus.

14. St. Victor I   189–198
African. The first Latin ecclesiastical writer; he demanded uniformity and discipline, especially regarding the celebration of Easter on the Sunday after Passover Day (fourteenth of Nisan).

15. St. Zephyrinus   198/199–217
Probably a Roman by birth. Criticized by the presbyter Hippolytus as weak, ineffective, and dependent upon his principal deacon, Callistus (who succeeded him).

16. St. Callistus I   217–222
Possibly Roman. A slave in his youth and sentenced to hard labor in Sardinia. Zephyrinus recalled him to Rome, but he was in conflict with his critic, Hippolytus; probably martyred.

17. St. Urban I   222–230
Possibly Roman. His reign fell squarely within the reign of Emperor Alexander Severus. Urban's grave slab is identified in the cemetery of Callistus.

18. St. Pontian   July 21, 230–September 28, 235*
Probably Roman. First pope to abdicate his office. He later died a martyr with the antipope Hippolytus.

19. St. Anterus   November 21, 235–January 3, 236
Greek. Another pontiff to be buried in the Cemetery of Callistus.

20. St. Fabian   January 10, 236–January 20, 250
Roman. Presided over prosperous church as energetic and respected administrator until Emperor Decius's persecutions began in 250. He was arrested and died in prison a martyr.

21. St. Cornelius   March 251–June 253

Roman. Elected after a fourteen-month vacancy. In the aftermath of the Decian persecutions, Cornelius faced the task of establishing policies for dealing with apostates from the faith.

22. St. Lucius I   June 25, 253–March 5, 254

Roman. Banished from Rome by Emperor Gallus, he returned under Emperor Valerian and dealt with heresies and the aftermath of persecutions.

23. St. Stephen I   May 12, 254–August 2, 257

Roman aristocrat. First to claim that pope is "Successor of St. Peter." Clashed with prominent Bishop Cyprian of Carthage over rebaptism of heretics, schismatics, and apostates.

24. St. Sixtus II   August 30, 257–August 6, 258

Greek. Attacked by Roman troops during a liturgical service and martyred.

25. St. Dionysius   July 22, 260–December 26, 268

Greek. Elected after two-year vacancy, during which the church was governed by council of presbyters; reorganized the local church and clarified church's doctrine of the Holy Trinity.

26. St. Felix I   January 5, 269–December 30, 274

Roman. One of the most obscure of the early popes; these dates are somewhat uncertain. He received a letter addressed to his predecessor and replied, a possible extract of which survives.

27. St. Eutychian   January 4, 275–December 7, 283

Born in Tuscany. Little reliable information about his pontificate is available. He was the last pope buried in the Cemetery of Callistus on the Appian Way.

28. St. Gaius [Caius]   December 17, 283–April 22, 296

Dalmatian. His reign occurred during a period of relative peace free from imperial persecution, which saw increased consolidation of organization and authority.

29. St. Marcellinus   June 30, 296–October 25, 304*

Possibly Roman. After Emperor Diocletian's edict against the church in 303, Marcellinus offered sacrifice to the Roman gods. He either abdicated or was deposed.

30. St. Marcellus I   May 27/June 26, 308–January 16, 309

Roman. Elected after longest vacancy to date (nearly four years). He imposed severe penalties against those who had compromised the faith during the Diocletian persecutions.

31. St. Eusebius   April 18, 309/310–October 21, 309/310

Greek. Controversies over apostasies during the Diocletian persecutions continued in his reign.

32. St. Miltiades [Melchiades]   July 2, 311–January 11, 314

Possibly African, more likely Roman. During his reign, Emperor Constantine issued edict of toleration and restoration of church properties, ending persecutions.

33. St. Sylvester [Silvester] I   January 31, 314–December 31, 335
Possibly Roman. One of the longest-serving popes, he did not attend Council of Nicea and presided in time of security.

34. St. Mark [Marcus]   January 18–October 7, 336
Possibly Roman. Very little known of his pontificate; donated his house for use as a church.

35. St. Julius I   February 6, 337–April 12, 352
Roman. A forceful champion of the Nicene Creed and the primacy of the Roman bishop.

36. Liberius   May 17, 352–September 24, 366
Roman. The first pope not to be canonized as a saint, he was considered weak because he capitulated to the Arian heresy in submission to the emperor. He later atoned for his error.

37. St. Damasus I   October 1, 366–December 11, 384
Born in Rome, about 305. First pope to enlist civil-military powers against his enemies. He strongly promoted papal primacy and commissioned the Vulgate Bible.

38. St. Siricius   December 384–November 26, 399
Roman. First bishop of Rome to employ the authority of "pope," as we now understand it.

39. St. Anastasius I   November 27, 399–December 19, 401
Roman. Embroiled in theological controversies, known for saintliness.

40. St. Innocent I   December 22, 401–March 12, 417
Roman. The son of his predecessor and one of the greatest early popes, he promoted primacy of the Roman See during political and military turmoil, including the attack on Rome by Alaric.

41. St. Zosimus   March 18, 417–December 26, 418
Greek, possibly of Jewish descent. Clashed with the African churches during a brief and turbulent pontificate.

42. St. Boniface I   December 28, 418–September 4, 422
Roman. Elected by substantial majority of Roman clergy and people, but disputed by Eulalius. Frail and elderly, he continued the struggle against the Pelagian heresy.

43. St. Celestine I   September 10, 422–July 27, 432
Italian. A vigorous, decisive pontiff; he continued to combat Pelagianism while facing yet another heresy, Nestorianism. Council of Ephesus held during his pontificate (431).

44. St. Sixtus III   July 31, 432–August 19, 440
Roman. Continued Celestine's policies and built the church of Santa Maria Maggiore.

45. St. Leo I   September 29, 440–November 10, 461
Roman. Known as Leo the Great; persuaded Attila the Hun not to overrun Rome (452); an advocate of the primacy of the pope and the dual human-divine natures of Jesus Christ.

46. Hilarus   November 19, 461–February 29, 468
Sardinian. Had been Leo's archdeacon and modeled his pontificate after the great pope.

47. St. Simplicius   March 3, 468–March 10, 483
Born in Tivoli, Italy. Opposed the Monophysite heresy; reigned during the fall of the western Roman Empire and the last western emperor in Rome.

48. St. Felix III   March 13, 483–March 1, 492
Roman. He was the first pope to submit his election to the emperor in Constantinople. He excommunicated the Eastern patriarch, beginning a thirty-five-year East-West schism.

49. St. Gelasius I   March 1, 492–November 21, 496
African. He had been archdeacon and right-hand man to Felix III. He forged a relationship with the Ostrogothic king of Italy against the East.

50. Anastasius II   November 24, 496–November 19, 498
Roman. Attempted to mend the East-West schism during his short pontificate.

51. St. Symmachus   November 22, 498–July 19, 514
Sardinian. Elected during a time of civil unrest in Rome, he was under the thumb of King Theodoric of Italy. First pontiff to award the pallium to a bishop outside of Italy.

52. St. Hormisdas   July 20, 514–August 6, 523
Born in Frosinone, Italy. Authored the *Forumula of Hormisdas,* which ended an East-West schism and established Rome as primatial apostolic see.

53. St. John I   August 13, 523–May 18, 526
Born in Tuscany. Ailing and aged when elected, he faced a resurgence of Arianism. First pope to leave Italy to travel to eastern capital of Constantinople.

54. St. Felix IV   July 12, 526–September 22, 530
Samnite by birth. Elected as the choice of Theodoric, the Ostrogothic king of Italy. Converted several Roman temples to Christian worship. Designated Boniface as his successor.

55. Boniface II   September 22, 530–October 17, 532
Gothic, born in Rome. Roman senate and clergy opposed his nomination by Felix as unconstitutional. His pontificate was tangled in political and dogmatic controversies.

56. John II   January 22, 533–May 8, 535
Mercury. Probably Roman. An elderly priest when elected, he was the first pope to change his name, since his given name was that of a pagan god. He reigned in a time of intense intrigue and instability.

57. ST. AGAPITUS I   May 13, 535–April 22, 536
Roman. An aristocrat and scholar who had opposed Felix's deathbed nomination of Boniface; he stood up to Emperor Justinian I. He died in Constantinople.

58. ST. SILVERIUS   June 1 or 8, 536–November 11, 537*
Born in Frosinone, Italy. The son of Pope Hormisdas, his was another relatively short pontificate, complicated by political intrigues. Deposed by imperial forces and died in exile.

59. VIGILIUS   March 29, 537–June 7, 555
Roman. He was considered a creature of Emperor Justinian and Empress Theodora. Presided during ongoing furor between Monophysite heretics and orthodox churchmen.

60. PELAGIUS I   April 16, 556–March 4, 561
Roman. He had participated in intrigues of previous two decades; not formally elected, but designated by emperor and reluctantly accepted by clergy of Rome and fellow bishops.

61. JOHN III   July 17, 561–July 13, 574
Roman. Had previously changed his name from Catelinus to John. He was favored by the emperor; while he was pope, Italy was invaded by the Lombards.

62. BENEDICT I   June 2, 575–July 30, 579
Roman. Waited nearly eleven months after election for imperial assent; requested emperor's help in securing Rome from siege by Lombards; ordained the future Gregory I as deacon.

63. PELAGIUS II   August 579–February 7, 590
Gothic, born in Rome. Elected during siege of Rome; dispatched Deacon Gregory to Constantinople. Saw Council of Toledo (589) and the growing rift between eastern and western patriarchs.

64. ST. GREGORY I   September 3, 590–March 12, 604
Roman aristocrat, born about 540. Possibly the greatest of all popes. Former prefect of Rome and cloistered monk; unanimously elected. He worked to revive Rome and papal authority.

65. SABINIAN   September 13, 604–February 22, 606
Born in Volterra, Tuscany. Served as Gregory's ambassador to court in Constantinople; unpopular among people of Rome in contrast to his successful, beloved predecessor.

66. BONIFACE III   February 19–November 12, 607
Greek, born in Rome. Waited a year for imperial mandate of election. Gregory's protégé and a successful diplomat, he held a synod to regulate the papal election process.

67. ST. BONIFACE IV   August 25, 608–May 8, 615
Born in L'Aquila. Waited ten months before confirmed by emperor. Faced plague and famine in Rome, and encouraged renewal of monasticism in the spirit of Gregory I.

68. St. Deusdedit [Adeodatus I]   October 19, 615–November 8, 618
Roman. Favored by anti-monastic, anti-Gregory forces. He focused on diocesan clergy of Rome, rather than on religious orders, and was known for his shrewdness.

69. Boniface V   December 23, 619–October 25, 625
Born in Naples. Waited thirteen months for imperial confirmation of election. Favored "secular" clergy versus religious; continued predecessors' support of the English church.

70. Honorius I   October 27, 625–October 12, 638
Born in Campania. He employed papal monks; had numerous political and doctrinal rivalries. First and only pope to be excommunicated by a council (Third Council of Constantinople, 680).

71. Severinus   May 28–August 2, 640
Roman. Elderly when elected, he waited twenty months for imperial confirmation. During his two-month pontificate, he raised the pay of Rome's secular clergy.

72. John IV   December 24, 640–October 12, 642
Dalmatian. Remained pope-elect for five months, awaiting imperial mandate. Focused on doctrinal issues that threatened schism between eastern and western churches.

73. Theodore I   November 24, 642–May 14, 649
Greek, born in Jerusalem. Attempted to eradicate the heresy of Monothelitism (which taught that Christ possessed a single, not a dual will) and perform good works in Rome.

74. St. Martin I   July 5, 649–June 17, 653*
Born in Todi, Umbria. Continued anti-Monothelite efforts at Lateran synod, in opposition to the emperor. Seized by imperial forces, tried, and deposed. Died from harsh imprisonment.

75. St. Eugene I   August 10, 654–June 2, 657
Roman. An elderly priest when elected during Martin's exile, he attempted to conciliate doctrinal controversies.

76. St. Vitalian   July 30, 657–January 27, 672
Born in Segni. Attempted to mend rift between Roman See and emperor in Constantinople and pressed for orthodox Easter dating (versus Celtic system).

77. Adeodatus II   April 11, 672–June 16, 676
Roman. An elderly monk when elected; quickly ratified by exarch (emperor's representative in Ravenna); stirred controversy with patriarch of Constantinople. Little else is known of him.

78. Donus   November 2, 676–April 11, 678
Roman. Also elderly and even more obscure than his predecessor. He evicted heretical Syrian monks from a Roman monastery and built and restored local churches.

79. ST. AGATHO   June 27, 678–January 10, 681

Sicilian. An active administrator, he convened synods and dispatched a delegation to the Council of Constantinople, but died before it concluded.

80. ST. LEO II   August 17, 682–July 3, 683

Sicilian. Waited eighteen months before receiving imperial approval of his election; reigned for less than a year; ratified and implemented the acts of the Council of Constantinople.

81. ST. BENEDICT II   June 26, 684–May 8, 685

Roman. Waited nearly a year after election for imperial mandate.

82. JOHN V   July 23, 685–August 2, 686

Syrian, born in Antioch. He had been one of Pope Agatho's representatives at the Council of Constantinople; he was severely ill throughout his year-long pontificate.

83. CONON   October 21, 686–September 21, 687

Thracian. A very controversial election, resulting in two antipopes. Conon was elderly, saintly, weak, and ailing.

84. ST. SERGIUS I   December 15, 687–September 8, 701

Syrian. Second pope in same year versus two antipopes. A strong administrator who clashed with Byzantine emperor, he reestablished some stability in the papacy.

85. JOHN VI   October 30, 701–January 11, 705

Greek. Reigned during deposition, then restoration, of eastern emperor Justinian II. Faced Lombard invasion of Italy.

86. JOHN VII   March 1, 705–October 18, 707

Greek. First pope who was son of a Byzantine political official, he complied with imperial wishes. Seen as weak; yet cultivated good relations with powerful Lombards in Italy.

87. SISINNIUS   January 15–February 4, 708

Syrian. Probably an elderly man when chosen, he was crippled with gout and served only twenty days.

88. CONSTANTINE   March 25, 708–April 9, 715

Syrian. Inherited problematic relationship with Byzantium and met with the emperor during a year-long journey outside of Rome. Asserted primacy of pope in ordination of bishops.

89. ST. GREGORY II   May 19, 715–February 11, 731

Roman, born 669. Former deacon, librarian, and diplomat. He protected orthodoxy, sent Boniface on a mission to Germany, and resisted Byzantine emperor's campaign against icons.

90. ST. GREGORY III   March 18, 731–November 28, 741

Syrian. Elected by acclamation, last pontiff to seek mandate of eastern emperor. He reigned during iconoclastic controversy and strengthened the church in England and northern Europe.

91. St. Zacharias [Zachary]   December 10, 741–March 22, 752
The last pope of Greek origin. Made peace with Lombards as well as Constantinople; supported claim of Pepin III (father of Charlemagne) to be king of the Franks.

92. Stephen III   March 26, 752–April 26, 757
Roman. Elected unanimously after four-day "reign" of Stephen II, who died before he could be consecrated as pope. Received Donation of Pepin, resulting in the beginning of the papal state.

93. St. Paul I   May 29, 757–June 28, 767
Roman. Younger brother of his predecessor, Stephen III; focused on strengthening the papal state and resisting iconoclasm of the east.

94. Stephen IV   August 7, 768–January 24, 772
Sicilian. He was a creature of powerful notary Christopher. Vacillated between the Lombards and the Franks; alienated Charlemagne, to the detriment of the papacy.

95. Hadrian [Adrian] I   February 9, 772–December 25, 795
Roman. Supported Charlemagne's reformation of Frankish church; saw relative peace in Italy; rebuilt economy of Rome; supported Second Council of Nicea's condemnation of iconoclasm.

96. St. Leo III   December 27, 795–June 12, 816
Roman. Elected unanimously. He survived attack by Roman mob. Christmas Day, 800, he crowned Frankish king as first Holy Roman emperor. Continued restoration of Rome.

97. Stephen V   June 22, 816–January 24, 817
Roman. Strengthened the papacy's relationship with the Holy Roman emperor, Louis I the Pious.

98. St. Paschal I   January 25, 817–February 11, 824
Roman. Abbot of a Roman monastery, he was quickly consecrated after election and then notified the emperor. An unpopular but strong pontiff.

99. Eugene II   May 824–August 827
Birthplace uncertain. He published *Roman Constitution*, which restored role of people and clergy of Rome in papal elections; required pope to take oath of loyalty to western emperor.

100. Valentine   August–September 827
Roman. Unanimously elected but reigned for approximately forty days.

101. Gregory IV   March 29, 828–January 25, 844
Roman. An aristocratic cardinal elected with support of the lay nobility of Rome; caught in conflict between family members for the Holy Roman throne and attempted to mediate.

102. Sergius II   January 844–January 27, 847
Roman. Elected by lay nobility and consecrated without the consent of Emperor Lothair. Dominated by his ambitious brother, he allowed simony to flourish.

103. St. Leo IV   April 10, 847–July 17, 855
Roman. Elected unanimously and consecrated without imperial approval. He vigorously governed the church and Rome; defended against Saracen threat; enforced church discipline.

104. Benedict III   September 29, 855–April 17, 858
Roman. Elected when the future Hardian II refused the office. Respected for his learning and piety; advised by the future Nicholas I; asserted Roman primacy over Constantinople.

105. St. Nicholas I   April 24, 858–November 13, 867
Born in Rome about 820. Elected after Hadrian refused election for a second time. Denied appointment of Photius as patriarch of Constantinople, which sparked another East-West schism.

106. Hadrian [Adrian] II   December 14, 867–December 14, 872
Roman, born in 792. Finally accepted election after death of Nicholas. He was considered imperious but ineffectual and, through vacillation, lost church of Bulgaria to Constantinople.

107. John VIII   December 14, 872–December 16, 882*
Roman. Became entangled in imperial-Frankish politics and crowned two emperors during his pontificate. First pope to be assassinated by members of his own court.

108. Marinus I   December 16, 882–May 15, 884
Born in Gallese, Tuscany. Significantly, as bishop of Caere, he was the first bishop of another see to be elected Roman pontiff (which had previously been forbidden).

109. St. Hadrian [Adrian] III   May 17, 884–September 885
Roman. Obscure pontificate; sought conciliation in ongoing rift with Constantinople.

110. Stephen VI   September 885–September 14, 891
Roman. Elected by laity and clergy of Rome, he was a reforming, political pope and was nearly deposed by the emperor.

111. Formosus   October 6, 891–April 4, 896
Probably Roman, born about 815. Diplomat, missionary, and bishop; previously excommunicated and exiled. Stephen VII put his corpse on trial (the "Cadaver Synod").

112. Boniface VI   April 896
Roman. Second-shortest pontificate on record; elected immediately after the death of Formosus, despite having been previously defrocked for immorality.

113. Stephen VII   May 896–August 897*
Roman. Bishop of Anagni; enemy of Formosus; his reaction to the Cadaver Synod resulted in his deposition. He was murdered in jail and his body thrown in the Tiber River.

114. ROMANUS   August–November 897*

Born in Gallese, Tuscany. Precise date of election unknown; pro-Formosus faction quickly deposed him.

115. THEODORE II   November 897

Roman. Elected to replace Romanus, he annulled the acts of the Cadaver Synod. Pontificate lasted only twenty days.

116. JOHN IX   January 898–January 900

Born in Tivoli. Although Sergius, bishop of Caere was elected, pro-Formosus party expelled him and elected John, with support of Italian king. He condemned the acts of the Cadaver Synod.

117. BENEDICT IV   February 900–July 903

Roman. Another pro-Formosus candidate, he was embroiled in imperial politics and crowned the "wrong man" as emperor, sending Rome into period of anarchy.

118. LEO V   August–September 903*

Born outside Rome, possibly in Ardea. Not a member of Roman clergy when elected. Probably a devout priest, he held office for about thirty days before he was murdered by his successor.

119. SERGIUS III   January 29, 904–April 14, 911

Roman. Elected pope for a second time amid controversies and violence; regarded the popes from John IX forward as interlopers and antipopes and continued anti-Formosus activities.

120. ANASTASIUS III   June 911–August 913

Roman. Probably a mild compromise candidate elected with support of Theodora the Elder of Rome; little is known of his pontificate.

121. LANDO   August 913–March 914

Born in Sabine territory, northeast of Rome. Very little is known of his short pontificate.

122. JOHN X   March/April 914–May 928*

Born in Tossignano. Archbishop of Ravenna. Elected with support of Theodora, his rumored mistress. Deposed by forces of Marozia, jailed, and suffocated to death in 929.

123. LEO VI   May–December 928

Roman. Elected when John X was still in jail, he was supported by Marozia, female dictator of Rome, and led a short, undistinguished pontificate.

124. STEPHEN VIII   December 928–February 931

Roman. Elected to succeed Leo when John was still imprisoned; undistinguished reign.

125. JOHN XI   March 931–December 935*

Roman, possibly illegitimate son of Pope Sergius III. Influenced by his mother, Marozia. Placed under house arrest by Alberic II, legitimate son and successor of Marozia.

126. Leo VII   **January 3, 936–July 13, 939**

Roman. Elected under influence of Alberic and served at the prince's sufferance.

127. Stephen IX   **July 14, 939–October 942**

Roman, born between 880 and 885. An honorable, pious man who fell out of favor with Prince Alberic II of Rome; he was imprisoned and mutilated, but not deposed before death.

128. Marinus II   **October 30, 942–May 946**

Roman. Owed election to Alberic; ineffective and subservient in the papacy.

129. Agapitus II   **May 10, 946–December 955**

Roman. Supported claim of Otto I to throne of Holy Roman Empire. On his deathbed, Alberic II extracted promise from clergy and Roman nobility to elect his son as pope.

130. John XII   **December 16, 955–May 14, 964***

Octavian. Born circa 937. Crowned Otto as emperor. One of the worst, most scandalous popes, he died of a stroke in bed with a married woman, after being deposed by Roman synod in 963.

131. Leo VIII   **Dec. 6, 963–March 1, 965**

Origin uncertain. The first layman to be pope, he was chief notary when elected. Installed by Otto I after John XII was deposed and after election of Benedict V was invalidated.

132. Benedict V   **May 22–June 23, 964***

Roman. A deacon known for holiness, he was elected after death of John XII against the emperor's wishes. He was eventually deposed and exiled to Hamburg.

133. John XIII   **October 1, 965–September 6, 972**

Roman, son of John Episcopus. Legitimately elected with support of emperor; imprisoned by Roman mob in December, 965, but escaped and served out his pontificate without interruption.

134. Benedict VI   **January 19, 973–July 974**

Son of Hildebrand, a Roman. Cardinal priest when elected as a reformer; waited four months for imperial approval. Imprisoned and strangled on orders of Boniface VII, antipope.

135. Benedict VII   **October 974–July 10, 983**

Roman aristocrat. Elected with imperial consent and support of noble Roman families; promoted monasticism and reigned during intermittent periods of civil upheaval.

136. John XIV   **December 983–August 20, 984**

Peter Canepanova, born in Pavia, Italy. Third pope to change his name (in this case, because it was the same as the first pope). A former imperial minister, he was uncanonically deposed by the antipope Boniface and starved to death in Castel Sant'Angelo prison.

137. JOHN XV   August 985–March 996
Roman, son of a priest named Leo. A cardinal priest elected after the death of antipope Boniface VII, he was supported by noble families and served their purposes.

138. GREGORY V   May 3, 996–February 18, 999
Bruno, a Saxon, born 972. The first German ever elected; he crowned Otto III as emperor, but fell out of favor and moved to Lombardy. He returned to Rome and imperial favor; died of malaria.

139. SYLVESTER [SILVESTER] II   April 2, 999–May 12, 1003
Gerbert, born in Auvergne, France, about 945. First French pope; "appointed" by the emperor, Otto III, was a reformer and proponent of papal prerogatives.

140. JOHN XVII   May 16–November 6, 1003
John Sicco, born in Rome. Possibly related to Crescentii family; short, obscure pontificate.

141. JOHN XVIII   December 25, 1003–July 1009*
John Fasanus, possibly Roman. Another pope elected at the behest of Roman dictator John II Crescentius; possibly abdicated and retired as a monk.

142. SERGIUS IV   July 13, 1009–May 12, 1012*
Peter (son of Peter), Roman. Changed his name out of respect for Peter the Apostle. Fate tied to Crescentii clan's declining fortunes; possibly deposed or killed.

143. BENEDICT VIII   May 18, 1012–April 9, 1024
Theophylact, born in Rome about 980. A layman, elected during period of unrest in Rome, rise of Tusculani family; crowned Henry II Holy Roman emperor; fought in sea and land battles.

144. JOHN XIX   April 19, 1024–October 20, 1032
Romanus Tusculan, younger brother of Benedict VIII. He achieved the papacy through bribes and family influence. Crowned Conrad II as Holy Roman emperor.

145. BENEDICT IX   October 21, 1032–July 17, 1048*
Theophylact Tusculan. He was forced out of office multiple times, reclaimed the papal throne, and was finally deposed in 1048. Excommunicated; he died in 1055 or 1056.

146. SILVESTER III   January 20–March 10, 1045*
John of Sabina. Bishop of Sabina. Crescentii family installed Silvester when Benedict was expelled from Rome; Benedict returned and exiled Silvester to a monastery. Died in 1063.

147. GREGORY VI   May 5, 1045–December 20, 1046*
John Gratian, probably Roman. Designated by Benedict as successor when the former abdicated in 1045; eventually deposed by a synod for crime of simony.

148. Clement II   December 25, 1046–October 9, 1047
Suidger, Saxon. The first of four successive "German" popes. First pope to remain bishop of another diocese, Bamberg. Crowned Henry III as Holy Roman emperor; possibly poisoned.

149. Damasus II   July 17–August 9, 1048
Poppo of Brixen, Bavaria. Nominated by the emperor upon Clement's death, he was the second pope to retain his diocese, Brixen. Died after only twenty-three days.

150. St. Leo IX   February 12, 1049–April 19, 1054
Bruno of Egisheim, born in Alsace June 21, 1002. Mutual excommunications by churches of Rome and Constantinople resulted in permanent schism between east and west.

151. Victor II   April 13, 1055–July 28, 1057
Gebhard of Dollnstein-Hirschberg, born in Swabia about 1018. Last of four German popes; continued reforms and steered papacy through turbulent imperial politics.

152. Stephen X   August 2, 1057–March 29, 1058
Frederick of Lorraine, French. Elected as reform compromise to a very brief pontificate.

153. Nicholas II   December 6, 1058–July 27, 1061
Gerard, born in Lorraine, France circa 1010. Bishop of Florence. Promoted Hildebrand (future Gregory VII) to archdeacon; reformed papal election process; issued anti-simony legislation.

154. Alexander II   September 30, 1061–April 21, 1073
Anselm, born in Baggio. Bishop of Lucca. Elected with support of Norman troops in Rome, he withdrew from the city during period of dispute; returned and became active reformer.

155. St. Gregory VII   June 30, 1073–May 25, 1085
Hildebrand, born in Tuscany about 1020. He transformed papacy with *Dictatus papae*, placing the pope above all powers, religious and secular. Excommunicated, then restored Emperor Henry IV. He died in exile.

156. Bl. Victor III   May 19, 1087–September 16, 1087
Daufer, probably born in Italy about 1027. Elected after lengthy vacancy; at first forced out of Rome, then returned and attempted a conciliatory, reforming direction for papacy.

157. Bl. Urban II   March 12, 1088–July 29, 1099
Odo, born in Châtillon-sur-Marne about 1035. Elected by acclamation in conclave, faced stand-off with emperor; declared first crusade for rescue of Jerusalem from Muslim forces.

158. Paschal II   August 14, 1099–January 21, 1118
Rainerius, born in Bieda di Galeata. Finally expelled the antipope Clement from Rome. He opposed lay investiture; had difficult, unpopular papacy.

159. GELASIUS II   March 10, 1118–January 28, 1119
John of Gaeta, Italy. A monk, author, and chancellor of Rome. He was imprisoned and fled the city to his native town, where he was consecrated pope. Died in exile in France.

160. CALLISTUS II   February 2, 1119–December 13, 1124
Guido, born in Burgundy about 1050. A strong personality and successful pope; continued opposition to investiture; excommunicated the emperor; jailed antipope.

161. HONORIUS II   December 21, 1124–February 13, 1130
Lamberto Scannabecchi, born in Imola. Fractious election led first to one pope then, in a quick reversal, to Lamberto. Pursued independent, reform-minded policies.

162. INNOCENT II   February 23, 1130–September 24, 1143
Gregorio Papareschi, born in Rome. Elected by a minority of cardinals that prompted election of antipope Anacletus. He governed church from France and Pisa; continued Gregorian reforms.

163. CELESTINE II   October 3, 1143–March 8, 1144
Guido of Città di Castello, Umbria. Unanimously elected as an elderly, experienced cardinal, with support of Empress Matilda.

164. LUCIUS II   March 12, 1144–February 15, 1145
Gherardo Caccianemici, born in Bologna, Italy. Chancellor and librarian of the church of Rome. Personally fought in assault on insurgent Romans; died of battle wounds.

165. BL. EUGENE III   February 18, 1145–July 8, 1153
Bernardo Pignatelli, born in Pisa, Italy. An abbot, elected on day of predecessor's death. First Cistercian pope. Preached the second crusade and vigorously pursued church reforms.

166. ANASTASIUS IV   July 12, 1153–December 3, 1154
Corrado, born in Rome, Italy. Elected on the day of his predecessor's death; took a conciliatory path in Roman politics and in relations with European kings and emperors.

167. HADRIAN [ADRIAN] IV   December 4, 1154–September 1, 1159
Nicholas Breakspear, English, born about 1100. The first and only English pope, he gave the king of England the right to incorporate Ireland into Britain.

168. ALEXANDER III   September 20, 1159–August 30, 1181
Orlando Bandinelli, born in Siena, Italy, circa 1100. Election politics caused schism during his pontificate. Convoked Third Lateran Council, requiring two-thirds majority for papal election.

169. LUCIUS III   September 1, 1181–November 25, 1185
Ubaldo Allucingoli, born in Lucca circa 1110. Weak and vacillating, spent his papacy living and governing from outside Rome.

170. Urban III   November 25, 1185–October 20, 1187
Umberto Crivelli, born in Milan, Italy. Archbishop of Milan, elected unanimously on the day of Lucius's death; an enemy of the emperor, but negotiated to secure papacy and papal state.

171. Gregory VIII   October 25–December 17, 1187
Alberto de Morra, born in Benevento about 1110. The elderly chancellor of the Roman church, he was elected with a mandate to seek imperial détente and reform clergy.

172. Clement III   December 19, 1187–March 1191
Paolo Scolari, born in Rome. Elected after conclave's first choice declined; returned papacy to Rome in 1188; negotiated political and ecclesiastical disputes; promoted third crusade.

173. Celestine III   April 14, 1191–January 8, 1198
Giacinto Bobo, born circa 1105 to aristocratic Roman family. Crowned Henry IV as Holy Roman emperor, tried to maneuver through the rough seas of international and Roman power politics.

174. Innocent III   February 22, 1198–July 16, 1216
Lothario, born in Agnani. Revolutionized the concept of the papacy itself as actively engaged in the naming and deposing of secular rulers and as the chief and only legislator of all matters relating to Catholic religious life. Convoked the historic Fourth Lateran Council and approved the foundation of the mendicant orders.

175. Honorius III   July 24, 1216–March 18, 1227
Cencio Savelli, Roman. Committed to a fifth crusade in the Holy Land; sent missionaries to Baltic countries; fought Moors in Spain as well as Albigenses in France.

176. Gregory IX   March 19, 1227–August 22, 1241
Ugo, born in Anagni about 1155. Prominent canon lawyer. Canonized St. Francis of Assisi and St. Dominic. Twice excommunicated Emperor Frederick II.

177. Celestine IV   October 25–November 10, 1241
Goffredo da Castiglione, ailing cardinal-bishop of Sabina. Elected after sixty-day conclave; lived for sixteen days thereafter, making his the third-shortest pontificate in history.

178. Innocent IV   June 28, 1243–December 7, 1254
Sinibaldo Fieschi, born in Genoa. Saw heightened conflict between papacy and imperial house; convoked First Council of Lyons; mired in nepotism and secular and financial concerns.

179. Alexander IV   December 12, 1254–May 25, 1261
Rinaldo, Count of Segni, nephew of Gregory IX, born in late twelfth century. Weak and indecisive with European power politics, sought reunification with eastern churches.

180. URBAN IV   August 29, 1261–October 2, 1264

Jacques Pantaléon, born in Troyes, France, about 1200. Increased size of college of cardinals, meddled in imperial and local politics, and pursued a potential end to East-West schism.

181. CLEMENT IV   February 5, 1265–November 29, 1268

Guy Foulques, born in Saint-Gilles-sur-Rhône, France, about 1195. Entered clergy as a widower. Supported French king against emperor; continued to seek end to East-West schism.

182. BL. GREGORY X   March 27, 1272–January 10, 1276

Tedaldo Visconti, born of nobility in Piacenza, about 1210. Elected as an arch-deacon; pursued crusade to reclaim the Holy Land, Second Council of Lyons, and reforms.

183. BL. INNOCENT V   January 21–June 22, 1276

Pierre of Tarentaise, born about 1224 in Savoy, France. First Dominican to be elected pope. A skilled theologian. Made steps toward rapprochement with the emperor and the king of Sicily.

184. HADRIAN [ADRIAN] V   July 11–August 18, 1276

Ottobono Fieschi, born in Genoa in 1205. Elected in tense conclave under influence of Charles of Anjou; suspended Gregory X's conclave rules, died after a month and a week as pope.

185. JOHN XXI†   September 8, 1276–May 20, 1277

Pedro Julião, born in Lisbon, circa 1210 to 1220. A physician and author; left papal government to Cardinal Orsini; pursued scholarly interests. Died after ceiling collapsed upon him.

186. NICHOLAS III   December 26, 1277–August 22, 1280

Giovanni Gaetano, born in Rome between 1210 and 1220. A member of the noble Orsini family; considered a statesman. Sought to increase papal influence in Italy.

187. MARTIN IV   March 23, 1281–March 28, 1285

Simon de Brie, born in Brion, France, circa 1210 to 1220. A very pro-French and anti-German pope, and a supporter of the Franciscan and Dominican mendicant orders.

188. HONORIUS IV   May 20, 1285–April 3, 1287

Giacomo Savelli, Roman aristocrat, born in 1210. The grand-nephew of Honorius III, preoccupied with the politics of Sicily; also extended the mendicant orders' privileges.

189. NICHOLAS IV   February 22, 1288–April 4, 1292

Girolamo Masci, born in Lisciano, Italy, September 30, 1227. The first Franciscan to become pope. He promoted missionary efforts in Asia, Africa, and Eastern Europe.

---

†There was no John XX, hence the numbering of the "Johns" is inaccurate.

190. St. Celestine V   August 29–December 13, 1294*
Pietro del Morrone, born in Molise, Italy, of peasant parents in 1209 or 1210. A Benedictine monk; he resigned papal office, was held captive, and died from harsh treatment at hands of his successor.

191. Boniface VIII   January 23, 1295–October 11, 1303
Benedetto Caetani, born in Anagni about 1235. A canon lawyer, he instituted the Holy Year in 1300, authored *Unam sanctum*, was captured by French troops, and died of trauma.

192. Bl. Benedict XI   October 22, 1303–July 7, 1304
Niccolò Boccasino, born in Treviso in 1240 of humble parentage. A Dominican and a relatively weak pope; he died of dysentery eight months after his election.

193. Clement V   June 5, 1305–April 20, 1314
Bertrand de Got, born in Villandraut, Gascony, in about 1260. He moved the papacy to France to escape the political and civil turbulence of Rome, becoming the first Avignon pope.

194. John XXII   August 7, 1316–December 4, 1334
Jacques Duèse, born in Cahors in 1244 of wealthy parents. The second Avignon pope, he inherited conflict with the Franciscan Spirituals as well as a complex political map.

195. Benedict XII   January 8, 1335–April 25, 1342
Jacques Fournier, born in Toulouse, circa 1280 to 1285. The third Avignon pope, a theologian and former inquisitor. A reformer, he oversaw construction of papal palace in Avignon.

196. Clement VI   May 7, 1342–December 6, 1352
Pierre d'Egleton, born in Maumont in 1291. The fourth Avignon pope, a noted preacher, patron of artists, and almsgiver; also famous for political-diplomatic intrigues and a luxurious court.

197. Innocent VI   December 18, 1352–September 12, 1362
Étienne Aubert, born in Monts in 1282. The fifth Avignon pope; he supported Dominicans, suppressed Franciscans, and promulgated Golden Bull regarding election of German king.

198. Bl. Urban V   November 6, 1362–December 19, 1370
Guillaume de Grimoard, born in Lozère in 1310. The sixth Avignon pope, a Benedictine monk who sought reunion between Rome and Constantinople and was beatified by Pius IX in 1870.

199. Gregory XI   January 4, 1371–March 27, 1378
Pierre Roger de Beaufort, born in Limoges in 1329. The seventh and last Avignon pope, also the last French pope; persuaded by St. Catherine of Siena to return seat of papacy to Rome.

200. URBAN VI   April 8, 1378–October 15, 1389
Bartolomeo Prignano, born in Naples about 1318. He proved to be a disastrous choice and the cardinals later declared him insane and the election invalid. Rebellious cardinals began the Great Schism.

201. BONIFACE IX   November 9,1389–October 1, 1404
Pietro Tomacelli, born in Naples in 1350. The second "Roman" pope during Great Schism; known for encouragement of nepotism in papal offices.

202. INNOCENT VII   October 17, 1404–November 6, 1406
Cosimo Gentile de' Migliorati, born in Sulmona, Abruzzi, Italy circa 1336. The third "Roman" pope during Great Schism; faced unrest in Rome and decline of support.

203. GREGORY XII   December 19, 1406–July 14, 1415*
Angelo Correr, born in Venice circa 1325. The last pope of "Roman" line during Great Schism; did not attend Council of Pisa, which elected yet a third pope. Abdicated as pope.

204. MARTIN V   November 21, 1417–February 20, 1431
Oddo Colonna, born in Gennazano, Italy, in 1368. Elected by extraordinary conclave held during Council of Constance to end forty-year Great Schism; he asserted that a council has no authority over a pope.

205. EUGENE IV   March 11, 1431–February 23, 1447
Gabriel Condulmaro, born in Venice, circa 1383. An Augustinian monk elected on promises of reform. Convoked Council of Basle, and worked toward reunion with Greek church.

206. NICHOLAS V   March 6, 1447–March 24, 1455
Tommaso Parentucelli, born in Sarzana, Italy, on November 15, 1397. Elected as a compromise over a Colonna family member, possessed reform ambitions, founded Vatican Library.

207. CALLISTUS III   April 8, 1455–August 6, 1458
Alfonso de Borgia, Spanish, born in Valencia on December 31, 1378. Uncle of future Pope Alexander VI, elected as compromise candidate; tried to organize crusade against the Turks.

208. PIUS II   August 19, 1458–August 15, 1464
Enea Silvio Piccolomini, born in Corsignano, October 18, 1405. An author, father of illegitimate children before taking orders, and diplomat; he died leading crusade against Turks.

209. PAUL II   August 30, 1464–July 26, 1471
Pietro Barbo, born in Venice, February 23, 1417. Influential cardinal nephew of Eugene IV; a promoter of carnivals and the arts, and a generally successful diplomat, died of a stroke.

210. SIXTUS IV   August 25, 1471–August 12, 1484
Francesco della Rovere, born in Celle on July 21, 1414. A Franciscan known for preaching, piety, and nepotism. A builder of Rome, including the Sistine Chapel and Vatican Library.

211. INNOCENT VIII   August 29, 1484–July 5, 1492
Giovanni Battista Cibò, born in Genoa in 1432, son of a Roman senator. Reign was plagued by insolvency and ineffective policies, leaving Rome and papal state in chaos.

212. ALEXANDER VI   August 26, 1492–August 18, 1503
Rodrigo de Borgia, born near Valencia, Spain, January 1, 1431. Possibly the most venal and corrupt pope ever. Placed church in hands of temporal European rulers.

213. PIUS III   October 1–18, 1503
Francesco Todeschini, born in Siena in 1439. Influential Renaissance cardinal and nephew of Pope Pius II, elected as compromise; was elderly and in ill health.

214. JULIUS II   November 1, 1503–February 12, 1513
Giuliano della Rovere, born in Albissola on December 5, 1443. Known as "warrior pope" for his political and military activities. He convoked Fifth Lateran Council, and patronized artists such as Michelangelo and Raphael.

215. LEO X   March 17, 1513–December 1, 1521
Giovanni de' Medici, born in Florence on December 11, 1475. Son of Lorenzo the Magnificent, he "packed" the college of cardinals with thirty-one new appointments in 1517.

216. HADRIAN [ADRIAN] VI   January 9, 1522–September 14, 1523
Adrian Florensz Dedal, born in Utrecht on March 2, 1459. A Dutchman, the last non-Italian pope until John Paul II; confronted Luther's early Reformation critique, as well as rise of Turks.

217. CLEMENT VII   November 19, 1523–September 25, 1534
Giulio de' Medici, born in Florence, May 26, 1479. Papacy threatened by Turkish advances in Eastern Europe and invasion of Italy by German emperor. Excommunicated Henry VIII.

218. PAUL III   October 13, 1534–November 10, 1549
Alessandro Farnese, born in Canino on February 29, 1468, of prominent Roman family. Despite being a keeper of mistresses and a nepotist, became a reformer. Convoked Council of Trent in answer to Protestant Reformation.

219. JULIUS III   February 8, 1550–March 23, 1555
Giovanni Maria Ciocchi del Monte, born in Rome on September 10, 1487. A canon lawyer and dean of the college of cardinals, he favored the reforms of the ongoing Council of Trent.

220. MARCELLUS II   April 10–May 1, 1555
Marcello Cervini, born in Montepulciano on May 6, 1501. The last pope to keep his baptismal name; died of a stroke after only twenty-one days as pope.

221. PAUL IV   May 23, 1555–August 18, 1559
Giampietro Carafa, born near Benevento on June 28, 1476, to noble Neopolitan family. Elected at age seventy-eight; established Index of Forbidden Books and confined Jews to Roman ghetto.

222. PIUS IV   December 25, 1559–December 9, 1565
Giovanni Angelo Medici, born in Milan on March 31, 1499. Elected during four-month conclave, he was a politically skilled pontiff who reconvened the Council of Trent.

223. ST. PIUS V   January 7, 1566–May 1, 1572
Michele Ghislieri, born in Bosco on January 17, 1504. A Dominican and former inquisitor, sought to implement Tridentine reforms and combat heresy. He excommunicated Elizabeth I.

224. GREGORY XIII   May 13, 1572–April 10, 1585
Ugo Boncompagni, born in Bologna, January 1, 1502, into a merchant family. A skilled administrator and supporter of the Counter-Reformation, responsible for Gregorian calendar.

225. SIXTUS V   April 24, 1585–August 27, 1590
Felice Peretti, born in Grottammare on December 13, 1520. Educated by Franciscans, he restored solvency of papal treasury and set number of cardinals at seventy.

226. URBAN VII   September 15–27, 1590
Giambattista Castagna, born in Rome on August 4, 1521. The shortest pontificate on record.

227. GREGORY XIV   December 5, 1590–October 16, 1591
Niccolò Sfondrati, born in Somma on February 11, 1535. Elected at a two-month conclave and plagued by ill health, he instituted episcopal and administrative reforms.

228. INNOCENT IX   October 29–December 30, 1591
Giovanni Antonio Fachinetti, born in Bologna on July 20, 1519. An experienced bishop, administrator, and former Patriarch of Jerusalem, he was favored by King Philip II of Spain.

229. CLEMENT VIII   February 3, 1592–March 3, 1605
Ippolito Aldobrandini, born in Fano on February 24, 1536. A church jurist and bureaucrat, and a pious, hard-working pontiff; supported continuing implementation of Tridentine reforms.

230. LEO XI   April 1–27, 1605
Alessandro Ottaviano de' Medici, born in Florence on June 2, 1535. The third Medici pope, elected at age seventy in frail health.

231. PAUL V   May 16, 1606–January 28, 1621
Camillo Borghese, born in Rome on September 17, 1552. A surprise compromise, elected at age fifty-two; placed Venice under papal interdict and lost diplomatic battles with France.

232. GREGORY XV   February 9, 1621–July 8, 1623
Alessandro Ludovisi, born in Bologna on January 9, 1554. First Jesuit-educated pope; expanded Vatican Library and Archives.

233. URBAN VIII   August 6, 1623–July 29, 1644
Maffeo Barberini, born in Florence, baptized on April 5, 1568. Drew papacy closer to France; his friend, Galileo Galilei, was censured during his pontificate.

234. INNOCENT X   September 15, 1644–January 7, 1655
Giambattista Pamfili, born in Rome on May 7, 1574. An experienced jurist, and advised by his sister-in-law, Olimpia Maidalchini. Supported missions to non-Christian countries.

235. ALEXANDER VII   April 7, 1655–May 22, 1667
Fabio Chigi, born in Siena on February 13, 1599. Continued predecessor's anti-French policies and became entangled in nepotism, awarding family members offices and estates.

236. CLEMENT IX   June 20, 1667–December 9, 1669
Giulio Rospigliosi, born in Pistoia on January 27, 1600. Spent relatively short pontificate on diplomatic and theological controversies.

237. CLEMENT X   April 29, 1670–July 22, 1676
Emilio Altieri, born in Rome on July 12, 1590. Elected at five-month-long conclave at age of seventy-nine, delegated day-to-day administrative control to a cardinal nephew-by-marriage.

238. BL. INNOCENT XI   September 21, 1676–August 12, 1689
Benedetto Odescalchi, born in Como on May 19, 1611. An austere, devout, experienced bishop and diplomat, faced difficult relations with French King Louis XIV; fought the Turkish threat.

239. ALEXANDER VIII   October 6, 1689–February 1, 1691
Pietro Ottoboni, born in Venice on April 22, 1610. A former inquisitor, elected with reluctant concurrence of French king; revived nepotism and luxurious style of papal court.

240. INNOCENT XII   July 12, 1691–September 27, 1700
Antonio Pignatelli, born in Bari on March 13, 1615. Devout and reform-minded, he reintroduced the austere policies of his namesake and instituted measures to improve quality of priests.

241. CLEMENT XI   November 30, 1700–March 19, 1721
Giovanni Francesco Albani, born in Urbino on July 23, 1649. Elected after factional and international maneuvering; coped with ongoing wars and Jansenism.

242. INNOCENT XIII   May 8, 1721–March 7, 1724
Michelangelo dei Conti (same family as Innocent III), born in Poli on May 13, 1655. An experienced curial operator; a relatively short and ineffective pontificate. Last pope to govern two sees at once.

243. BENEDICT XIII   May 29, 1724–February 21, 1730
Pietro Francesco Orsini, born in Gravina on February 2, 1649. An aristocrat; a Dominican friar who continued to live as such; concerned with poor and sick; an ineffective, unpopular pope.

244. CLEMENT XII   July 12, 1730–February 6, 1740
Lorenzo Corsini, born in Florence on April 7, 1652. Elected at advanced age, went blind after two years as pope; presided during decline in papal prestige and international power.

245. BENEDICT XIV   August 7, 1740–May 3, 1758
Prospero Lorenzo Lambertini, born in Bologna on March 31, 1675. Elected in longest conclave of modern times; improved finances and security of papal state, put a moderate face on papacy.

246. CLEMENT XIII   July 6, 1758–February 2, 1769
Carlo della Torre Rezzonico, born in Venice on March 7, 1693. Elected after a French veto in the conclave; a strongly pro-Jesuit pope, ordered Sistine nudes covered.

247. CLEMENT XIV   May 28, 1769–September 22, 1774
Giovanni Vincenzo Antonio Ganganelli, born in Sant'Arcangelo, on October 31, 1705. A Franciscan, elected in controversial conclave; issued bull that suppressed the Society of Jesus.

248. PIUS VI   February 22, 1775–August 29, 1799
Giovanni Angelo Braschi, born in Cesena on December 25, 1717. Enmeshed in papal dignities and protocols, he became a prisoner of Napoleon and died away from Rome.

249. PIUS VII   March 14, 1800–August 20, 1823
Luigi Barnabà Chiaramonte, also born in Cesana, April 14, 1742. Of noble birth, a surprisingly strong pope; suffered harsh indignities under Napoleon's bullying, restored the Society of Jesus.

250. LEO XII   September 28, 1823–February 10, 1829
Annibale della Genga, born in Castello della Genga, August 22, 1760. Elected as a pastoral pope and became embroiled in politics and diplomacy.

251. PIUS VIII   March 31, 1829–November 30, 1830
Francesco Saverio Castiglione, born in Cingoli on November 20, 1761. Elected in poor health and served for less than two years.

252. GREGORY XVI   February 2, 1831–June 1, 1846
Bartolomeo Alberto Cappellari, born in Belluno, Venetia, on September 18, 1765. An austere scholar and monk; rejected rationalism and religious freedom, but denounced slavery.

253. BL. PIUS IX   June 16, 1846–February 7, 1878
Giovanni Maria Mastai-Ferretti, born in Senigallia on May 13, 1792. Longest papacy on record. Defined the Immaculate Conception of the Blessed Virgin Mary; convoked the First Vatican Council, which defined the infallibility of the pope.

254. LEO XIII   February 20, 1878–July 20, 1903
Gioacchino Vincenzo Pecci, born in Carpineto on March 2, 1810. Elected as "caretaker," but survived for a quarter-century; wrote influential encyclical *Rerum novarum*, on workers' rights.

255. ST. PIUS X   August 4, 1903–August 20, 1914
Giuseppi Melchiorre Sarto, born in Riese on June 2, 1835. From peasant stock, known as an energetic bishop, considered religiously, rather than politically, focused.

256. BENEDICT XV   September 3, 1914–January 22, 1922
Giacomo Della Chiesa, born in Genoa on November 21, 1854. An experienced papal diplomat; pope during World War I; eased opposition to Modernism; worked for post-war reconciliation.

257. PIUS XI   February 6, 1922–February 10, 1939
Ambrogio Damiano Achille Ratti, born in Desio, May 31, 1857. A scholar and librarian, forged Lateran Treaty that created modern Vatican City State. First pope to broadcast on radio.

258. PIUS XII   March 2, 1939–October 9, 1958
Eugenio Maria Giuseppi Giovanni Pacelli, born in Rome, on March 2, 1876. One of the most accomplished and controversial of popes; pontiff during World War II and early Cold War. First pope to appear on television.

259. BL. JOHN XXIII   October 28, 1958–June 3, 1963
Angelo Giuseppi Roncalli, born in Sotto il Monte, on November 25, 1881. Startled the world by convoking the Second Vatican Council (1962–65); beloved pastoral figure.

260. PAUL VI   June 21, 1963–August 6, 1978
Giovanni Battista Montini, born in Concesio, Italy, on September 26, 1897. An intellectual and experienced bureaucrat; continued the work of Vatican II; expanded college of cardinals.

261. JOHN PAUL I   August 26–September 28, 1978
Albino Luciani, born in Forno di Canale on October 17, 1912. First pope born in twentieth century and first to take a double name. Substituted simple installation ceremony for coronation.

262. JOHN PAUL II   October 16, 1978–April 2, 2005
Karol Wojtyla, born in Wadowice, Poland, on May 18, 1920. The first non-Italian in 455 years; revolutionized papacy though his deep faith. Likely to be remembered as "John Paul the Great."

263. BENEDICT XVI   April 19, 2005–

ANTIPOPES

St. Hippolytus	217–235
Novatian	251–258
Felix II	355–November 22, 365
Ursinus	September 366–November 367
Eulalius	December 27, 418–April 3, 419
Lawrence	November 22, 498–February 499 (501–505)
Dioscorus	September 22–October 14, 530
Theodore	687
Paschal	687
Constantine II	July 5, 767–August 6, 768
Philip	July 31, 768
John	January 844
Anastasius Bibliothecarius	August–September 855
Christopher	September 903–January 904
Boniface VII	June–August 974 and August 984–July 20, 985
John XVI	February 997–May 998
Gregory	May–December 1012
Benedict X	April 5, 1058–January 1059
Honorius II	October 28, 1061–May 31, 1064
Clement III	June 25, 1080, March 1084–September 8, 1100
Theodoric	September 1100–January 1101
Albert	1102
Silvester IV	November 18, 1105–April 12, 1111
Gregory VIII	March 8, 1118–April 1121
Celestine	1124
Anacletus II	February 14, 1130–January 25, 1138
Victor IV	March–May 29, 1138
Victor IV[†]	September 7, 1159–April 20, 1164
Paschal III	April 22, 1164–September 20, 1168
Callistus III	September 1168–August 29, 1178
Innocent III	September 29, 1179–January 1180
Nicholas V	May 12, 1328–July 25, 1330
Clement VII	September 20, 1378–September 16, 1394
Benedict XIII	September 28, 1394–July 26, 1417
Alexander V	June 26, 1409–May 3, 1410
John XXIII	May 17, 1410–May 29, 1415
Clement VIII	June 10, 1423–July 26, 1429
Benedict XIV	November 12, 1495
Felix V	November 5, 1439–April 7, 1449

[†]Duplications of names sometimes occurred in cases of antipopes.

NOTES

INTRODUCTION

1. LeMoyne College-Zogby survey, reported by Catholic News Service, October 2003.

2. John Paul II, *Ut unum sint*, no. 92.

3. Ibid., no. 94.

4. See *Selecting the Pope: Uncovering the Mysteries of Papal Elections* by Greg Tobin (Barnes & Noble Publishing, 2003) for details on the history and development of the conclaves.

5. Eamon Duffy, *Saints and Sinners: A History of the Popes* (New Haven: Yale University Press, 1997), p. 13.

CHAPTER 1: "TU ES PETRUS" (CIRCA A.D. 30–1198)

1. Gregory VII, *Dictatus Papae*, cited in Brian Tierney, *The Crisis of Church and State: 1050–1300* (Hasbrouck Heights, N.J.: Prentice-Hall, 1964), p. 89.

CHAPTER 2: THE POPE AS RULER AND REFORMER (1198–1846)

1. Innocent III, "Sermon on the Consecration of a Pope," in Tierney, op. cit., p. 237.

2. Boniface VIII, *Unam sanctum*, in Tierney, op. cit., p. 366.

3. Paul III, *Sublimus Deus*, cited in Colman J. Barry, *Readings in Church History* (Westminster, Md.: Newman Press, 1960), p. 179.

4. Frank J. Coppa, *The Modern Papacy Since 1789* (New York: Addison Wesley Longman, 1998), p. 33.

5. J.N.D. Kelly, *Oxford Dictionary of Popes* (Oxford: Oxford University Press, 1986), p. 308.

6. Richard McBrien, *Lives of the Popes: The Pontiffs from St. Peter to John Paul II* (San Francisco: HarperCollins, 1997), p. 336.

CHAPTER 3: THE UNIVERSAL PASTOR (1846–1978)

1. John Farrow, *Pageant of the Popes* (New York: Sheed and Ward, 1942), p. 452.

2. Pius IX, *Quanta cura*, cited in Kelly, op. cit., p. 310.

3. McBrien, op. cit., p. 347.

4. Kelly, op. cit., p. 311.

5. McBrien, op. cit., p. 364.

CHAPTER 4: POPE JOHN PAUL II (1978–2005)

1. George Weigel, *Witness to Hope* (New York: HarperCollins, 1999), p. 863.

2. Ibid, p. 849.

3. Excerpt is taken from the official Web site of the Holy See: http://www.vatican.va/

4. Excerpted from Zenit News Agency.

CHAPTER 5: THE CONCLAVE

1. Translation quoted with permission of Catholic News Service, April 18, 2005.

2. Translation quoted with permission of Catholic News Service, April 20, 2005.

CHAPTER 6: YOUNG JOSEPH

1. Direct quotes from Joseph Ratzinger are taken from his autobiography: Joseph Ratzinger, *Milestones: Memoirs 1927–1977* (San Francisco: Ignatius Press, 1998).

2. Mark Landler and Richard Bernstein, "A Future Pope Is Recalled: A Lover of Cats and Mozart, Dazzled by Church as a Boy," *New York Times*, April 22, 2005.

CHAPTER 7: PRIEST AND SCHOLAR

1. Joseph Ratzinger and Vittorio Messori, *The Ratzinger Report* (San Francisco: Ignatius Press, 1985).

2. Direct quotes from Joseph Ratzinger are taken from his autobiography: Joseph Ratzinger, *Milestones: Memoirs 1927–1977* (San Francisco: Ignatius Press, 1998).

Chapter 8: From Council to Episcopacy

1. Joseph Ratzinger, *Milestones: Memoirs 1927–1977* (San Francisco: Ignatius Press, 1998).

2. Ratzinger and Messori, op. cit., p. 19.

3. Rev. Thomas Guarino, S.T.D., interview with Michael Barone, Immaculate Conception Seminary, April 22, 2005.

4. Petra Krishok and Craig Whitlock, "Muted Enthusiasm in Homeland," www.washingtonpost.com, April 20, 2005.

Chapter 9: The Congregation

1. Cindy Wooden, "Pope Benedict likes verbal sparring, thinks God has sense of humor," Catholic News Service, April 21, 2005.

2. A general source used throughout this chapter regarding Ratzinger's approach to various issues was: Brian Donohue, "A Look at the Social Views of the New Pope" *The Newark Star-Ledger*, April 24, 2005.

3. Ratzinger and Messori, op. cit., p. 19.

4. Ratzinger and Messori, op. cit., p. 21.

5. Joseph Ratzinger and Peter Seewald, *Salt of the Earth: The Church at the End of the Century*, (San Francisco: Ignatius Press, 1997).

6. Jerry Filteau, "Cardinal McCarrick says leaked Ratzinger memo is not whole story," Catholic News Service, July 4, 2004.

Chapter 10: The State of the World and the Church

1. Pope John XIII, Opening Address to Second Vatican Council, October 11, 1962, cited in Walter M. Abbot, S.J., general editor, *The Documents of Vatican II* (New York: The America Press, 1966), page 712.

2. Paul Johnson, *A History of Christianity* (New York: Atheneum, 1976), p. 508.

3. Laurie Goodstein, "Catholics in America, A Restive People," *The New York Times*, April 3, 2005.

4. Zenit News Service, May 23, 2004.